The Killing of Mr Toad
David Gooderson

finboroughtheatre

First published in the United Kingdom in 2009 by Finborough Theatre, 118 Finborough Road, London, SW10 9ED
admin@finboroughtheatre.co.uk | www.finboroughtheatre.co.uk

A CIP record for this book is available from the British Library.

ISBN: 978-0-9560869-1-4

Cover Design: Rebecca Maltby
Cover Image: E. H. Shepard © The estate of E. H. Shepard reproduced with permission of Curtis Brown.

Printed by Polprint, 63 Jeddo Road, London, W12 9EE, UK.
Telephone +44-(0)20-8749-0777. e-mail print@polprint.co.uk

D2 & Co in association with Neil McPherson
for the **finborough**theatre presents

The Killing of Mr Toad

by David Gooderson

finboroughtheatre

First performance at the Finborough Theatre, London:
Sunday, 19 April 2009

The Killing of Mr Toad
by David Gooderson

Cast in order of appearance

Elspeth Grahame	**Elizabeth Counsell**
Rat	**Stefan Bednarczyk**
Mole	**Jeffrey Perry**
Badger	**Timothy Davies**
Toad	**Leo Conville**

The living-room of Elspeth Grahame's house in Pangbourne, Berkshire.

A few minutes during June 1934.

The events of the play are true.

There will be one interval of fifteen minutes.

The performance lasts approximately two hours.

Our patrons are respectfully reminded that, in this intimate theatre, any noise such as rustling programmes, talking or the ringing of mobile phones may distract the actors and your fellow audience-members.

Interval drinks may be ordered in advance from the bar.

Director	**David Gooderson**
Designer	**Ruth Hall**
Musical Director	**Stefan Bednarczyk**
Choreographer	**Miranda Fellows**
Sound Designer	**Giles Webb**
Lighting Designer	**Chris Withers**

Stefan Bednarczyk Rat / Musical Director
Theatre includes *The Game Of Love And Chance* (National Theatre and Tour), *Laughter On The 23rd Floor* (Queen's Theatre and National Tour), *The LA Plays* (Almeida Theatre), *The Devil Wears Tweed, The Mystery of Edwin Drood,* and *Young Dick Barton* (Warehouse Theatre, Croydon), *ZIP!* (National Tour), *The Glee Club* (Bush Theatre), *Semi-Monde* (Lyric Theatre), *The Jermyn Street Revue* (Jermyn Street Theatre), *Whenever* (Stephen Joseph Theatre, Scarborough), *Five O'Clock Angel* (Edinburgh Festival, Hampstead Theatre and King's Head Theatre).

Solo Cabaret Performances include seasons at Pizza on the Park, King's Head Theatre, New End Theatre, Jermyn Street Theatre and overseas in Cannes, Antibes, Monaco, San Francisco, New York, Los Angeles, Barbados, Vienna and Adelaide.
Film includes *Composed, Sea Change, Friends Pictured Within*, and *Topsy-Turvy.*
Television includes *EastEnders, Crocodile Shoes, Crown Prosecutor, Love Hurts, Harry Enfield and Chums.*

Leo Conville Toad
At the Finborough Theatre, Leo played Private Syd Sommers in *Red Night* in 2005.
Trained at the University of Birmingham and Arts Educational Schools.
Theatre includes Mole in *The Wind in the Willows, A Midsummer Night's Dream, Henry IV Part One, Camelot, The Taming of the Shrew* and *Babe* (Open Air Theatre, Regent's Park), *Kolbe's Gift* (Greater London Tour), *The Searcher* (Greenwich Theatre), *The Ugly Duckling* (Stephen Joseph Theatre, Scarborough), *Forgotten Voices from the Great War* (Pleasance London), *The Seagull* (National Theatre Studio), *The Rivals* (British Actors' Company Tour), and *The Ramayana* (Birmingham Rep).
Film includes *Terrible Times Today.*
Television includes *Holby Blue* and *The Bill.*
Radio includes *The Dark is Rising.*

Elizabeth Counsell Elspeth Grahame.
At the Finborough Theatre, Elizabeth played Harmony Blueblossom in *The Beautiful People* in 2008.
Theatre includes *Much Ado About Nothing, The Three Sisters, As You Like It,* and *Dear Liar* (Bristol Old Vic), *Pygmalion* and *The Beaux Strategem* (Theatre Royal Windsor), *Macbeth* – opposite Michael Gambon – and *St Joan* (Forum Theatre, Billingham), *Present Laughter* (Vaudeville Theatre), *M Butterfly* (Shaftesbury Theatre), *The Corn is Green* (Old Vic), *Jean Seberg* (National Theatre), *Salad Days* (Vaudeville Theatre), *Noel and Gertie* (Jermyn Street Theatre), *Valentine's*

Day (Globe Theatre), *101 Dalmatians* (Nuffield Theatre), *The Glass Menagerie* (Lyric Theatre, Belfast), *The Haunted Hotel* (National Tour), *An Inspector Calls, The Birthday Party* (Theatr Clwyd), and *Park Avenue* (Sadler's Wells). She was also Michael Redgrave's leading lady in *Shakespeare's People* touring South America and Canada. Television includes *ER, Lock Stock, Nelson's Column, Executive Stress,* and 37 episodes of *Brush Strokes*

Timothy Davies Badger
Read Modern Languages at Cambridge University.
Theatre includes *María de Buenos Aires* (Bath Theatre Royal and Buxton Opera House), *Quartermaine's Terms* (Northampton Theatre Royal and Salisbury Playhouse), *Heartbreak House* (Chichester Festival Theatre), *Lysistrata* (The Old Vic and Wyndham's Theatre), *The Lady from Maxim's, Plenty, Man and Superman,* and *The Oresteia* (National Theatre), *The Taming of the Shrew, Julius Caesar,* and *Faust* (Royal Shakespeare Company), *Twelfth Night* (English Shakespeare Company), *Antony and Cleopatra* (Shakespeare's Globe), and *Bedroom Farce* (Prince of Wales Theatre).
Film includes *Perfume: The Story of a Murderer* and *Mysteries of Egypt.*
Television includes *Filth: The Mary Whitehouse Story, Fantabulosa!, A Touch of Frost, Survival of the Fittest, The Hitch Hiker's Guide to the Galaxy* and the title role in *Kilvert's Diary.*

Jeffrey Perry Mole
Trained at the Guildhall School of Music and Drama
Theatre includes *The Dybbuk, The Ordeal of Gilbert Pinfold, Huckleberry Finn, Twelfth Night, Have You Anything to Declare?* (Royal Exchange Theatre, Manchester), *Prisoner Cell Block H – The Musical* (Queen's Theatre), *Sugar* (West Yorkshire Playhouse), *You Can't Take it With You,* and *Nashville* (King's Head), *Forgotten Voices of The Great War* (Southwark Playhouse and The Pleasance), *The Dock Brief and Edwin* (Orange Tree Theatre, Richmond), *Love's A Luxury, Time and Time Again, All For Mary,* and *Strictly Murder* (The Mill at Sonning), *Hobson's Choice, Equus,* and *Measure For Measure* (Salisbury Playhouse), *All My Sons* (Liverpool Playhouse), *Hamlet, Spokesong,* and *The School For Scandal* (Leicester Haymarket), *Salad Days* (Nottingham Playhouse), *Playing Sinatra, Hard Times,* and *Hysteria* (Not The National Theatre), *Habeas Corpus* (National Tour), and *When We Are Married* (National Tour).
Television includes *Poirot, Rumpole, The Bill, Love in a Cold Climate, Rather You Than Me, About Face, The Bag Lady, Micawber, Too Much Sun, The Tripods, Five Children and It, The Lion The Witch and The Wardrobe, Unnatural Causes, There's A Viking in my Bed,* and *Crime Travellers.*

David Gooderson Playwright and Director
Studied Law and English at Cambridge University where he was a leading member of Footlights. As an actor, he is best known for his television work which includes Davros in *Dr Who* (BBC) and Simpkins the Pathologist in *A Touch of Frost* (ITV). His writing includes four plays broadcast on BBC Radio 4 and five plays for children, co-written with David Conville and all produced at the Open Air Theatre, Regent's Park, including a musical adaptation of *The Wind in the Willows* (with music by Carl Davis) which has twice broken Box Office records, and played two Christmas seasons in the West End. He also edited *My Dearest Mouse*, a facsimile edition of Grahame's letters to his son. Directing includes*The Playboy of the Western World* with Stephanie Cole (Salisbury Playhouse), and Staff Direction for English Touring Opera. In September 2006, he directed the premiere of his latest play *Kolbe's Gift* (Greater London Tour). In March 2009 he gave a talk about Kenneth Grahame at the British Library as part of a special event to celebrate the centenary of *The Wind in the Willows*. www.david-gooderson.co.uk

Ruth Hall Designer
At the Finborough Theatre, Ruth designed *Captain Oates' Left Sock* and was Associate Designer on *Country Magic*. She trained at the Royal Welsh College of Music and Drama, and the Royal Shakespeare Company's Postgraduate Apprenticeship in Design. Designs includes *Kindertransport* (Aberystwyth Arts Centre and Welsh Tour), *The Fetch* (Old Red Lion), *Three More Sleepless Nights* and *Fourplay* (Tristan Bates Theatre), *Café Cariad* (Welsh Tour with the National Youth Theatre of Wales), *The School for Wives* and *Topless Mum in Dead Hero Shocker* (Tobacco Factory, Bristol). As an Assistant Designer, she has worked on *Zorro The Musical* (Garrick Theatre), *Henry VI, Parts I, II* and *III*, *Romeo and Juliet*, *The Tempest*, *The Winter's Tale*, and *Pericles* (Royal Shakespeare Company).

Miranda Fellows Choreographer
Trained at Elmhurst Ballet School. Theatre includes *Hello Dolly* (Theatre Royal Drury Lane and National Tour), *Promises Promises* (Prince of Wales Theatre and Broadway), *Relatively Speaking* (US National Tour), *Stepping Out* (Duke of York's Theatre and National Tour) *No No Nanette* (Theatre Royal Drury Lane), *Hans Andersen* (London Palladium), *Very Good Eddie* (Piccadilly Theatre), *Pal Joey* (Albery Theatre), *Mr and Mrs* (Palace Theatre), *A Midsummer Night's Dream* and *Much Ado About Nothing* (Open Air Theatre, Regent's Park), *Toad of Toad Hall* (The Old Vic, Piccadilly Theatre, Duke of York's Theatre etc), *Kafka's Dick* (Piccadilly Theatre), *La Cage Aux Folles, 42nd Street,* and *Follies* (Wimbledon Theatre) and *The Pirates of Penzance,* and *Dames at Sea* (Cannizarro Open Air Theatre).

Rick Perrins Stage Manager
Taught Theatre Studies and ran the Drama Department at Esher College. Theatre includes *Dead Man Walking* (National Tour), *Kolbe's Gift* (Greater London Tour) and *Golden Opportunities* (Croydon Warehouse). He also writes theatre reviews for *Whatsonstage.*

finboroughtheatre

"One of the most stimulating venues in London, fielding a programme that is a bold mix of trenchant, politically thought-provoking new drama and shrewdly chosen revivals of neglected works from the past." *The Independent*

"A disproportionately valuable component of the London theatre ecology. Its programme combines new writing and revivals, in selections intelligent and audacious." *Financial Times*

"A blazing beacon of intelligent endeavour, nurturing new writers while finding and reviving neglected curiosities from home and abroad" *The Telegraph*

The multi-award-winning Finborough Theatre – led by Artistic Director Neil McPherson – presents both plays and music theatre, concentrated exclusively on new writing and rediscoveries of neglected works from the 19th and 20th centuries. We also run a Resident Assistant Director Programme and a vibrant Literary Department. The Finborough Theatre won the Empty Space Peter Brook Mark Marvin Award in 2004, and was the inaugural winner of the Empty Space Peter Brook Award's Dan Crawford Pub Theatre Award in 2005 which it also won again in 2008. Neil McPherson was named Best Artistic Director in the 2009 *Fringe Report* Awards. The Finborough Theatre was the only unfunded theatre to be awarded the prestigious Pearson Playwriting Award bursary for Chris Lee in 2000, Laura Wade in 2005, James Graham in 2006, Al Smith in 2007 and Anders Lustgarten in 2009 – as well as the Pearson Award for Best Play for Laura Wade in 2005 and James Graham in 2007.

Founded in 1980, artists working at the theatre in the 1980's included Clive Barker, Rory Bremner, Nica Burns, Kathy Burke, Ken Campbell and Clare Dowie. In the 1990's, the Finborough Theatre became particularly known for new writing including Naomi Wallace's first play *The War Boys*; Rachel Weisz in David Farr's *Neville Southall's Washbag*; four plays by Anthony Neilson including *Penetrator* and *The Censor*, both of which transferred to the Royal Court Theatre and new plays by Tony Marchant, David Eldridge, Mark Ravenhill and Phil Willmott. New writing development included Mark Ravenhill's *Shopping and F***king* (Royal Court, West End and Broadway), Conor McPherson's *This Lime Tree Bower* (Bush Theatre) and Naomi Wallace's *Slaughter City* (Royal Shakespeare Company).

Since 2000, New British plays have included Laura Wade's London debut with her adaptation of W.H. Davies' *Young Emma*, commissioned specially for the Finborough Theatre; Simon Vinnicombe's *Year 10* which went on to play at BAC's *Time Out* Critics' Choice Season; James Graham's *Albert's Boy* with Victor Spinetti; Joy Wilkinson's *Fair* which transferred to the West End; and Nicholas de Jongh's *Plague Over England*, currently playing in the West End. London premieres have included Jack Thorne's *Fanny and Faggot* which also transferred to the West End. Many of the Finborough Theatre's new plays have been published and are available to purchase from our website.

UK premieres of foreign plays have included Brad Fraser's *Wolfboy*; Lanford Wilson's *Sympathetic Magic*; Larry Kramer's *The Destiny of Me*; Tennessee Williams' *Something Cloudy, Something Clear*; Frank McGuinness' *Gates of Gold* with William Gaunt and the late John Bennett in his last stage role (which also transferred to the West End); Nilo Cruz's *Hortensia and the Museum of Dreams* with Linda Bassett; the English premiere of Robert McLellan's Scots language classic, *Jamie the Saxt*, and Joe DiPietro's *F***king Men*, currently playing at the King's Head Theatre.

Rediscoveries of neglected work have included the first London revivals of Rolf Hochhuth's *Soldiers* and *The Representative*; both parts of Keith Dewhurst's *Lark Rise to Candleford*; *The Women's War* – an evening of original suffragette plays; *Etta Jenks* with Clarke Peters and Daniela Nardini; *The Gigli Concert* with Niall Buggy and Paul McGann; Noël Coward's first play, *The Rat Trap*; Charles Wood's *Jingo* with Susannah Harker; and the sell-out production of Patrick Hamilton's *Hangover Square*.

Music Theatre has included the new (premieres from the UK and USA by Grant Olding, Charles Miller, Michael John LaChuisa, Adam Guettel, Andrew Lippa and Adam Gwon) and the old (the sell-out Celebrating British Music Theatre series, reviving forgotten British musicals).

Visit us at **www.finboroughtheatre.co.uk** or join us at MySpace, Facebook, YouTube and Twitter.

finboroughtheatre

118 Finborough Road, London SW10 9ED
admin@finboroughtheatre.co.uk | www.finboroughtheatre.co.uk
Artistic Director | Neil McPherson
Resident Designer | Alex Marker
General Manager | Anna Bartholomew
Pearson Playwright-in-Residence | Anders Lustgarten
Playwrights-in-Residence | James Graham, Al Smith, Laura Wade, Alexandra Wood
Literary Associate | Titas Halder
Resident Casting Director | Rachel Payant
Technical Director | Oliver Luff
Resident Assistant Directors | Ellie Browning, Ben Kidd, Tim Newns
Interns | Joanna Daniel, Jessi James, Sarah Loader, Becky Novak, Jake Orr, Eilís Sanfey

The Finborough Theatre has the support of the Pearson Playwrights' Scheme
Sponsored by Pearson PLC.

The Finborough Theatre is a member of
The Independent Theatre Council and Musical Theatre Matters UK

Mailing – Please email admin@finboroughtheatre.co.uk or give your details to our Box Office staff to join our free mailing list. If you would like to be sent a free season leaflet every three months, just include your postal address and postcode.

Feedback – We welcome your comments, complaints and suggestions. Do email the Artistic Director at neilmcpherson@finboroughtheatre.co.uk or write to Finborough Theatre, 118 Finborough Road, London SW10 9ED.

Friends – The Finborough Theatre is a registered charity. We receive no public funding, and rely solely on the support of our audiences. Please do consider supporting us by becoming a member of our Friends of the Finborough Theatre scheme. There are four categories of Friends, each offering a wide range of benefits. Richard Tauber Friends – Charles Lascelles. Lionel Monckton Friends – Anonymous. William Terriss Friends – Leo Liebster. Peter Lobl.

Smoking is not permitted in the auditorium and the use of cameras and recording equipment is strictly prohibited.

In accordance with the requirements of the Royal Borough of Kensington and Chelsea:
1. The public may leave at the end of the performance by all doors and such doors must at that time be kept open.

2. All gangways, corridors, staircases and external passageways intended for exit shall be left entirely free from obstruction whether permanent or temporary.
3. Persons shall not be permitted to stand or sit in any of the gangways intercepting the seating or to sit in any of the other gangways.

The Finborough Theatre is licensed by the Royal Borough of Kensington and Chelsea to The Steam Industry, a registered charity and a company limited by guarantee. Registered in England no. 3448268. Registered Charity no. 1071304. Registered Office: 118 Finborough Road, London SW10 9ED. The Steam Industry is under the Artistic Direction of Phil Willmott. www.philwillmott.co.uk

Production Acknowledgements

Assistant Director | Ellie Browning

Stage Manager | Rick Perrins

Press Representative | Neil McPherson press@finboroughtheatre.co.uk

Graphic Design | Rebecca Maltby

Associate Producer | Deirdre Gooderson

The Killing of Mr Toad

David Gooderson

Characters
Elspeth Grahame
Rat
Mole
Badger
Toad

Place: The living-room of Elspeth Grahame's house in Pangbourne, Berkshire.

Time: A few minutes during June 1934.

Author's Note
I was given a biography of Kenneth Grahame in the mid 1970's and a glance at the faded dust jacket was enough to show that here was rich dramatic material. My subsequent research led me beyond the biographies to hunt for the family papers – which at first no one could find. They were thought to be at Dorneywood (formerly owned by Elspeth Grahame's brother, and now a ministerial country residence), but researches revealed nothing except a few books and Alastair Grahame's photograph album – hidden behind the squash courts.

I eventually discovered that the papers had been sold to the Bodleian Library in Oxford. There I found everything that Elspeth had decided to keep including letters to her from various mediums and all Kenneth's courtship letters – about a hundred of them in neat pencil, all coyly misspelt ("fanx orfly" etc). The omissions were almost as telling: none of Elspeth's side of the correspondence, and nothing from Alastair's career at Rugby, Eton or Oxford.

I was too late to contact most of Alastair's contemporaries, but I did manage to trace the boy who shared a study with him at Rugby, one of the many he couldn't stand. The "boy" was now a delightful, chain-smoking 78 year old, still working as a solicitor in Lincoln's Inn. I spent a fascinating day with him and his help was invaluable.

The play is as faithful to the facts as I could make it.

The Killing of Mr Toad was first performed at the Cricklade Theatre, Andover, as part of a Southern Arts tour on 21 September 1982 and subsequently at Salisbury Playhouse in October 1982 with the following cast:

Elspeth Grahame	**Ann Windsor**
Rat	**Michael Lunts**
Mole	**Peter Robert Scott**
Badger	**Kevin Moore**
Toad	**Emlyn Harris**
Directed by David Conville	

It was subsequently performed at the King's Head Theatre, London from 18 August 1983 with the following cast:

Elspeth Grahame	**Deborah Norton**
Rat	**John Warner**
Mole	**Robert Austin**
Badger	**Hugh Sullivan**
Toad	**Rupert Graves**
Directed by Peter Watson	

The play was later adapted for radio and was first broadcast on BBC Radio 4 on 30 December 1984 with the following cast:

Elspeth Grahame	**Barbara Jefford**
Kenneth Grahame	**Edward Hardwicke**
Alastair Grahame	**Stephen Garlick**
Alastair Grahame as a child	**Susan Sheridan**
Rat	**John Warner**
Badger	**Geoffrey Matthews**
Figgis	**Colin Starkey**
Miss Noyce	**Narissa Knights**
Miss Parker	**Tessa Worsley**
Doctor	**John Webb**
Official	**Brian Smith**
Clayton	**William Hope**
Prefect	**Michael Jenner**
Coroner	**David Garth**
Directed by Richard Wortley	

ACT ONE

A room in semi-darkness. A gracious 1930's room: piano and piano-stool; small writing desk or davenport; chaise longue and footstool; beside them a table with a drawer in it; on the table a photograph; two upright chairs; a standard lamp, a large lugubrious potted plant, armchair and large pile of newspapers; the debris of an untidy person scattered round the chaise. French windows, with heavy curtains drawn.

ELSPETH GRAHAME, an old woman well-preserved mentally and physically and well-spoken despite her shabby appearance, is noisily asleep on the chaise longue, feet on footstool and a rug pulled up under her chin. She wears a long dressing gown concealing the fact that she is fully dressed underneath. There is a knock on the front door.

ELSPETH: *(Half asleep)* Who is it?
(Knocking again – louder)
(Getting up) Alright, I'm coming.
(More knocking – louder still)
Alright!
(Exit. Sound of the front door opening)

ELSPETH'S VOICE: Now the next time this happens...
Where's he gone? Couldn't you wait five seconds! Come back, you little reptile!

(Sound of the front door slamming. ELSPETH re-enters with a small bunch of flowers) Waking me up in the middle of the afternoon and just dropping them on the doorstep. Delivery boys! They get worse and worse.

(She switches on the standard lamp: dingy light)

Oh they're lovely!

(She looks round for a vase; sees a mug, which contains tea-leaves from the night before; empties them over the plant; puts the flowers in the mug beside the photograph)

They shall have the place of honour.

(Examining the card that came with them)

They're from a child, a little child! *(She addresses the photograph)* Listen, Dino. "Dear Mrs Grahame, *The Wind in the Willows* is my favourite story. I hope these flowers will comfort you, as I know you are unhappy. Love from Penelope. (aged 9)". Isn't that *sweet*? Two years, and I'm still getting letters! They love you, my Dino. The little children love you. You made them so happy.

(*From behind the chaise she produces an enamel jug half-full of water.*)

You made everyone happy.

(*She pulls a china bowl from under the chaise and pours some water*)

Kings, Presidents, Prime Ministers – even the dreary old Kaiser. The whole world united in your praise!

(*She notices a paper-bag containing a chicken drumstick on the table by the photograph. She takes out the chicken and smells it.*) If only one didn't have to eat.

(*She slams down the chicken and removes her woolly bedsocks*)

Not that one can go on eating at today's prices. Fresh salmon half-a-crown per pound! Can't afford to sniff it! Frightful, perfectly frightful.

(*She sits, her feet in water*)

If only one didn't have to wash.

(*She picks up the chicken again and eats without enthusiasm*)

What am I doing here? I'm like an old drumstick. Picked clean and fit for the dustbin. Ugh!

(*She puts the chicken down again. As she takes her handkerchief out of her dressing-gown pocket to wipe her fingers, she pulls out an unopened letter. She examines it.*)

When did this arrive? Posted last Thursday? I'm going potty! (*Opening it*) Huh! Old Milly Parker again. I wonder if she's had a message. (*She reads for a moment*) Oh God, this is impossible! Her handwriting is worse than the doctor's. "This is one of the days I can't spell". That is the understatement of the century. (*Reads for a moment*) Not much of interest. The usual exhortations to buy the *Psychic News* – "Physic News" she calls it. "I do think it would be best if you went to see a medium yourself." Don't think I haven't tried, Milly dear. The best I could manage was a weird old man in Sloane Square who cost a fortune and kept insisting that the spirits wouldn't come out because it was too foggy. If a medium requires fine weather, one may as well abandon the search in England. (*Skimming the letter.*) Usual guff about the late lamented Bert. " Yesterday I saw him carrying mistletoe and waving." Clever old Bert carrying mistletoe on midsummer day. "Then I saw".... It can't be. (*Suddenly attentive*) "Then I saw *Mouse* and your husband – yes, I really did. Mouse showed himself with a..." What's this?...her writing!.. Looks like muffler "twisted round his neck. He says you are not to worry, he is well and happy; he always... loved you, but now he *worships* you". My darling boy! " He says you must be happy for Mr Toad's sake. All the animals insist that you look after yourself and eat properly." Of course I shall! "Mouse and your husband were loaded with flowers of all sorts – the name 'Elspeth' in big letters, no doubt about that name. Both smiled as I held out arms to take their gifts. They were so real, I quite forgot.

(*She looks up and gazes at the flowers imagining they are the flowers in the letter*) They're beautiful... (*Reading the letter again*) "Be sure our dear ones are near us. It's only our stupid lack of faith that prevents us from seeing and hearing them". (*She sinks back on the chaise*) I wonder... I wonder.

(*She puts down the letter and picks up the chicken drumstick. She eats in a desultory manner for a moment, then softly sings to herself, to the tune of 'The Church's One Foundation' [Aurelia])*

> He has crossed a wider river
> Than otter or vole can swim,
> And the Master of Life, the Lover
> Of Beauty, has welcomed him

(*Eating more hungrily*) It was like a fairy-tale. A real life fairy-tale. The famous author and the little boy. The famous author tiptoes into the night-nursery, slips an arm about a little night-gowned boy and tells him a story. A bedtime story that will become world famous! My husband! My son! Oh Dino, I'm so proud!

(*She sings triumphantly now, conducting with her drumstick.*)

> And the children that dwell in glory
> Have captured a gentle soul;
> They are crowding round for the story
> Of Ratty and Toad and Mole.

And Badger ...

(*Re-wrapping the remains of the chicken drumstick and replacing it carefully in the paper bag.*)

Mustn't forget gruff old Badger, keeping them all in order, telling them what's what.

(*Drying her feet with a towel.*)

Those little animals on the heady heights of Parnassus! Among the immortals! It doesn't seem possible! Even after their famous victory over the weasels. I wonder how they're taking to it. Mole must be dreadfully excited. And Ratty – dear Ratty – such a gentleman – is he still messing about in boats?...

(*Enter RAT, with a large picnic hamper. He wears an open-necked shirt, canvas trousers and yachting cap as in "The Wind in the Willows", but is completely human: no mask, or tail or fur. He throws open the curtains in front of the French windows; sunlight streams in.)*

RAT: Come on, Moly. Do hurry up.

MOLE: (*entering*) Coming Ratty. Coming.

(MOLE wears a black velvet smoking suit, almost hidden by a large whitewash-splashed apron, as in "The Wind in the Willows": but he too has no animal fur etc.)

RAT: Give us a hand with the luncheon-basket.

MOLE: (*helping him*) This is better than whitewashing!

(Removing his apron) Hang spring-cleaning, that's what I say!

RAT: So do I.

MOLE: (*jumping on apron*) Bother whitewash!

RAT: Absolutely.

MOLE: This is spring without the cleaning! Oh Ratty, what a day I'm having!

(RAT dabbles his fingers in an imaginary river. MOLE peers at it)

So – this – is – a river!

RAT: *The* river.

(RAT mimes unfastening a rope and stepping into a boat)

MOLE: And you really live by the river?

RAT: By it and with it and on it and in it. (*Settles himself and picks up imaginary oars)* It's my world and I don't want any other. Now then, step lively.

(MOLE gingerly climbs into the 'boat' and sits opposite RAT, who starts to scull.)

MOLE: Do you know, I've never been in a boat before in all my life?

RAT: What? Never been in a – you never – well I never – what have you been doing then?

MOLE: Is it so nice as all that?

RAT: Nice? It's the *only* thing. Believe me, there is nothing, absolutely nothing half so much worth doing as simply messing about in boats. You're always busy, and you never do anything in particular. And when you've done it, there's always something else to do; and you can do it if you like, but you'd much better not.

MOLE: What a jolly life!

RAT: (*dreamily*) Simply messing...messing about...in boats...

MOLE: Look ahead, Rat! The bank!

(*RAT falls backwards, heels in the air.*)

(*RAT and MOLE 'freeze'. Throughout the previous scene ELSPETH has been reclining with eyes half-closed, seeing the 'animals' in her mind's eye*)

ELSPETH: (*chuckling*) The dreamer! The joyous oarsman! They're so like you, my Dino. The same innocence. The same indolence. (*New thought*) The same love of food...

(*RAT and MOLE 'unfreeze'*)

RAT: (*picking himself up*) Here's our backwater at last.

(*MOLE, wriggling with curiosity, points to the hamper.*)

MOLE: What's inside it?

RAT: Just a trifle of lunch. Cold tongue cold ham cold beef pickled gherkins salad French rolls cress sandwiches potted meat ginger beer lemonade soda water – nothing special.

MOLE: (*ecstatic*) This is too much!

RAT: Do you really think so? It's only what I always take on these little excursions; and the other animals are always telling me I'm a mean beast and cut it very fine.

MOLE: Can we start now?

RAT: By all means.

(*They unpack the hamper. The objects removed could be real or imaginary and this could apply to all the other objects that occur in ELSPETH'S imaginings*)

MOLE: Oh my! German sausage!... Garibaldi biscuits!...Military pickle!...

RAT: Pitch in old fellow.

MOLE: What lies over there?

RAT: That? Oh, that's just the Wild Wood. We don't go there much, we river-bankers.

MOLE: Aren't they – aren't they very nice people in there?

RAT: We-ell the squirrels are alright, and the rabbits – some of 'em - though rabbits are a mixed lot. But- there- are- others...

MOLE: Others?

RAT: Oh I'm very good friends with them, pass the time of day when we meet, and all that; but they..... break out sometimes. Badger's alright. He lies right in the heart of it – wouldn't live anywhere else, if you paid him. Dear old Badger! Nobody interferes with *him*. They'd better not.

MOLE: And beyond the Wild Wood? Where it's all blue and dim?...

RAT: Beyond the Wild Wood comes the Wide World.

MOLE: The Wide World? Whatever's that?

(*RAT and MOLE 'freeze'*)

ELSPETH: (*sharply*) That's something that doesn't matter, either to you or me.

(*RAT and MOLE 'unfreeze'.*)

RAT: I've never been there, and I'm never going. Nor you either, if you've any sense at all.

(*RAT and MOLE 'freeze'.*)

ELSPETH: Don't ever refer to it again, please!

(*RAT and MOLE 'unfreeze'.*)

RAT: (*lying down*) I wonder which of us had better pack the luncheon-basket.

MOLE: Oh, please let me.

RAT: Of course. If you insist.

MOLE: (*starting to pack the basket*) It's all so exciting! The sparkle...and the ripple...(*sniffs*) and the scents...and the sunlight! I'll have a little rest on this pile of old leaves.

(*He sits on the pile of old newspapers in the corner of the room. They begin to move underneath him*)

MOLE: (*being rocked*) What...a day...I'm...having! Oh my!

Oh my!

(*He is dislodged and BADGER appears*)

BADGER: Now the *very* next time this happens, I shall be exceedingly angry. I will *not* have people sitting down on me as if I were part of the furniture. Who is it *this* time? Speak up!

RAT: Why it's Mr Badger.

BADGER: H'm company. These crowds.

(*He stumps upstage to the French windows*)

RAT: That's just the sort of fellow he is. Simply hates Society.

(*The three animals 'freeze'.*)

ELSPETH: (*to herself*) They're all so like you. You poured yourself into all your creation. Well not all. Mr. Toad is the exception that proves the rule. He's quite different...

(*The animals 'unfreeze'.*)

BADGER: Where is he?

(*Sound of a motor-car approaching at high speed*)

TOAD: (*off – calling*) Hello, you fellows! This is the life, eh?

(*The car stops noisily.*)

RAT: It's Toad!

MOLE: Good old Toady!

(*The car backfires loudly*)

BADGER: Oh unhappy Toad!

(*TOAD appears arrayed in motoring goggles, cap, gauntlets and enormous overcoat – and human, like the others*)

TOAD: Sorry I'm late, you chaps, but I've had rather a busy morning. Escaped from prison, dressed as a washerwoman – devilish cunning disguise, what? – jumped a train, swam a river, stole a motor-car and 'poop-poop' here I am!

(*He swaggers round the stage, driving an imaginary car and humming loudly. RAT shakes his head. MOLE laughs. ELSPETH applauds.*)

MOLE: Escaped from prison! You clever, ingenious Toad!

BADGER: Don't encourage him, you'll only make him worse.

(*The four animals 'freeze'. ELSPETH turns to BADGER.*)

ELSPETH: But he is *so* like my little one. (*To herself again*) To think, my darling, you even left me a picture of my own little son. Exaggerated, of course, but oh so life-like...

(*The animals 'unfreeze'.*)

TOAD: (*Singing*)

> The world has held great heroes,
> As history books have showed,
> But never a name to go down to fame,
> Compared with that of ....Toad!

BADGER: Toad! You boastful, puffed-up animal! It's not you we're celebrating, it's.....

ELSPETH: K.G.!

BADGER: Precisely.

TOAD: Sorry, Mr.Badger, sir – I mean your majesty, your magnificence...

BADGER: That will do. I'm sorry, ma'am, if this low animal has inconvenienced you in any way. We were, as I was trying to intimate before I as so rudely interrupted –

TOAD: *Fearfully* sorry, Mr. Badger.

BADGER: Be silent! We were about to sing the praises of your creator, Mr...

ELSPETH: Kenneth Grahame!

BADGER: The same. A small entertainment in his honour. I trust you approve.

ELSPETH: We'll sing songs! We'll play the gramophone! Like we did in the old days.

BADGER: Your wish is our command. Rat, to the pianoforte!

RAT: (*saluting*) Badger!

(*RAT goes to piano. TOAD leaps up on a chair.*)

TOAD: Song by Toad! Words and music by Toad! From an Original Idea by Toad! Performed by – the Author.

BADGER, MOLE and RAT: (*reprovingly*) Toad!

TOAD: With a little help from his friends.

(*He jumps down and stands beside BADGER*)

(*SONG: to the tune of 'Toad's Song' from 'Toad of Toad Hall'. [music by H. Fraser-Simson])*)

BADGER: The clever men at Oxford
              Have every kind of degree

TOAD: But which of them came to win such fame

ALL:	As *popular* Mr. G.
RAT:	The President in the White House The Kaiser in his yacht at sea,
TOAD:	And who was their choice? Was it Freud, was it Joyce?
ALL:	*(spoken)* No! It was Mr. G.
BADGER:	*(dramatically – to chords)* The children were shut in the nursery The grown-ups had got the key
RAT:	*(dramatically – to chords)* But who gave the shout
TOAD:	"Let them out, let them out!"
ALL:	*(shouted)* Revolutionary Mr.G.!
MOLE:	*(sings – sentimentally)* He was the children's champion In all the works he penned
BADGER:	Oh how they cried
TOAD:	Sent flowers when he died
ELSPETH:	*(spoken)* K.G. the children's friend!
ALL:	*(sung in harmony)* K.G.,the children's friend!
ELSPETH:	*(applauding)* That was splendid! Splendid! But haven't we missed out a verse?
RAT:	Have we?
ELSPETH:	About a Very Important Person.
MOLE:	Who?
ELSPETH:	Who married the man, who sired the boy, who inspired the tale – that you are!
TOAD:	Who?
BADGER:	Listen.

ELSPETH: (*spoken to chords*)
A lady sat at her window
Waiting patiently.

RAT: She cried:

ELSPETH: Look, who's that *handsome* man!

RAT: They answered:

ALL: (*as if introducing a star*)
Mis-ter G!

(*RAT and BADGER gesture towards MOLE, who looks startled.*)

ELSPETH: (*dreamily*) Tall...dashing...captain of the fifteen...
A god among men!

MOLE: Does she mean me?

ELSPETH: Yes you, my modest Dino.

TOAD: Moly as K.G.? Simple little Mole as *my* creator?

BADGER: As your great-uncle, the Archdeacon, might have said – had he lived – in every man of stature there is a shy little animal crying to be let out. Let Mole play his part. And you play yours – later.

(*MOLE immediately starts to sob*)

TOAD: What's the matter, Moly? Don't you want to do it?

MOLE: (*tearful in a theatrical way*) My mother died when I was five years old! Papa turned to drink and couldn't look after us! We left our lovely home in Scotland and were sent to a grandmother in England - four hundred miles away!

RAT: What *is* all this?

MOLE: (*switching off 'tears' like a tap*) I'm K.G., aren't I?
Well, I'm beginning at the beginning!

BADGER: We don't want any of that, Mole.

ELSPETH: We certainly do not. This is a celebration not some ghastly Freudian analysis.

MOLE: Sorry.

(*Drumroll on the piano. MOLE takes off his jacket and flexes his muscles like a strong man*)

RAT: Pillar of the Bank of England!

(*Chord on the piano. MOLE stands like Samson holding up the temple. Everyone applauds.*)

BADGER: Famous author!

(*Chord on the piano. MOLE stands, holding up the temple with one hand and writing furiously with the other.*)

ELSPETH: That's the idea!

TOAD: *Pagan Papers.*

(*Chord. Applause*)

RAT: *The Golden Age.*

(*Chord. Applause*)

TOAD: *Dream Days.*

(*Chord. Applause*)

BADGER: *The Headswoman.*

(*Silence*)

ELSPETH: (*anxiously*) The Headswoman?

BADGER: (*lightly*) About a female executioner. (*ELSPETH is agitated*)

She cuts people's heads off. (*ELSPETH is more agitated*)

Only in fun.

ELSPETH: Of course! His only story about grown-ups. A charming

piece of nonsense.

RAT: And in his spare time...

(*"Scotland the Brave" [Trad.] on piano. MOLE marches up and down*)

BADGER: The London Scottish.

TOAD: Rank of Sergeant.

ELSPETH: Ogled by nursemaids.

(*"Country Gardens" [Trad.] on piano*)

RAT: Toynbee Hall, Stepney.

TOAD: (*posh voice*) Culture for the working – classes.

(*MOLE rolls up his sleeves*)

BADGER: Boxing.

(*MOLE 'boxes'*)

RAT: Fencing.

(*MOLE 'fences'*)

TOAD: Billiards.

(*MOLE 'plays' billiards*)

ELSPETH: Lectures on literature – to prospective charwomen!

(*TOAD, RAT and BADGER put on headscarves. MOLE coughs, prepares to speak*)

TOAD, RAT, BADGER: *(singing to the tune of "Men of Harlech" [Trad.])*
What is one among so many?

TOAD: Can I go and spend a penny?

BADGER: Don't mind'er, we loves yer Kenn-ee!

TOAD, RAT, BADGER: All we want's a kiss!

(*They hurl themselves on MOLE*)

ELSPETH: (*rising*) Don't!

(*Silence. The 'animals' stand back*)

He's mine!

(*Slinky, stripper-type version of "You Made me Love You". ELSPETH vamps round MOLE, removing her dressing-gown and throwing it to BADGER. She peels off the old, frayed cardigan. She is now revealed in an elegant 1890s dress or costume. Sound of Victorian front-door bell. Music stops abruptly. ELSPETH stands facing MOLE, who is now KENNETH GRAHAME.*)

MOLE/KENNETH: I'm sorry to trouble you, but my name's Grahame.
I wonder if I might have a word with Mr Fletcher-Moulton.

ELSPETH: I'm afraid he's out at the moment. Can I help?

KENNETH: I doubt it. It's a business matter concerned with the Bank of England. Dull stuff I'm afraid.

ELSPETH: Well, come in anyway. Would you care for some tea?

KENNETH: (*looking at watch*) Well I really ought not to spare the time...

ELSPETH: But you will.

KENNETH: Thank you.

ELSPETH: Allow me to introduce myself. I'm Elspeth Thomson,
Mr Fletcher-Moulton's step-daughter.

KENNETH: And I'm Kenneth Grahame.

ELSPETH: Not *The* Kenneth Grahame, of *Pagan Papers* fame?

KENNETH: I'm afraid so.

ELSPETH: You must think me dreadful not recognising you.

KENNETH: Not at all.

ELSPETH: Do sit down.

KENNETH: Thank you.

(*They sit on upright chairs placed behind them, where they stand, by BADGER and TOAD*)

ELSPETH: Well this has made my day, Mr. Grahame.

KENNETH: The pleasure is mine, Miss Thomson.

ELSPETH: You know, it's almost uncanny. Ever since I was a child, famous authors have been drawn to me. Tennyson was.

KENNETH: Tennyson? How did you come to know him?

ELSPETH: We met on holiday at Pontresina. We were great friends.

KENNETH: You and Tennyson?

ELSPETH: I was 10 and he was 63. And when I was 8, Mark Twain came to call. My parents were out, so I received him – in the nursery! "Will you take tea" I said. "Tea?" he replied, "I only drink whisky." So I ran downstairs with the teapot and told the butler to fill it with whisky. And Mr. Twain drank it – neat! But don't you try it, Mr. Grahame. As an expert on childhood, it wouldn't be the thing.

KENNETH: Even though I'm a Scot?

ELSPETH: How *do* you find the time to write *and* be a pillar of the Bank of England?

KENNETH: I'll let you into a secret, Miss Thomson. I have a red ledger in which I scribble. Not all my scribbles are strictly financial.

ELSPETH: During office hours?

KENNETH: It has been known.

ELSPETH: You write so wonderfully about children, Mr. Grahame, dare I ask how many you have?

KENNETH: Oh I'm a bachelor. One of the secrets of my success is that I make it a rule not to spend too much time being entertained by charming young ladies. (*Standing up*). So now, if you'd excuse me, I must be getting back to the bank.

ELSPETH: (*Standing up*) Well, you shall come to one of my soirees. Only the most distinguished writers and artists are invited.

KENNETH: I shall be honoured to be included. Goodbye, Miss Thomson.

ELSPETH: Au revoir, Mr. Grahame.

(*KENNETH moves away. The chairs are whisked back.*)
(SONG: – to the tune of "*Polly Perkins of Paddington Green*" [Trad.])

RAT: *She – was – as –* beautiful as a butterfly
           With an intellect rare
           (*ELSPETH acknowledges the compliments*)

TOAD: Was thirty-six-year-old Miss Thomson
           (*ELSPETH gives TOAD a look*)

TOAD, RAT, BADGER:
           Of smart Onslow Square.
           (*Meanwhile ELSPETH does a dainty dance*)

BADGER: She was hostess for her step-dad, a judge and M.P.

TOAD: Entertaining the paragons of societ-ee;

BADGER: The rich and respectable their compliments paid,

RAT: But unless she got a firm proposal she'd die an old maid.

TOAD: She – was – as – sociable as a butterfly
           But in need of a beau,

RAT: And now at last she'd caught a big fish

TOAD, RAT, BADGER:
           (*spoken*) Was not letting go!
           (*ELSPETH holds out her hand. KENNETH steps forward.*
           She takes his arm. He looks slightly embarrassed.)

BADGER: He – was – as – eminent as Tennyson
           And as nice as his books

TOAD: With such a perfect combination

TOAD, RAT, BADGER:
           Of charm and good looks.

           (*Meanwhile ELSPETH and KENNETH do a little
           pas-de-deux.*)

RAT: For a year they were a-courting,
           Though hardly on fire.

TOAD: But then had to separate,
           A spur to desire.

BADGER: In Cornwall he convalesced after pneu-mon-i-ah
                  She had to stay in London looking after Papa....

*(KENNETH goes to one side of the stage, ELSPETH goes to the other.
Lighting change: KENNETH and ELSPETH are in separate pools of light.
TOAD, RAT and BADGER slip out)*

ELSPETH: 36 Onslow Square, 6th June 1899. My darlin' Dino. I'm sending
you another food parcel, 'cos I'm worried 'bout what you eatin'.This German
man who know everyfing 'bout diet, say if you follow 'is rules you be really
'ealthy like people in Berlin. So be a good boy an' eat it all up! – or Minkie'll
be very cross! An' I'm sendin' you an umbrella an' a nice woolly muffler. Oh
Dino, I've a shockin' sin to confess! Last time I forgot to put mustard in the
pasties! Write soon, my pet.

KENNETH: Fowey Hotel, Fowey, Cornwall. My dearest Elspeth...

ELSPETH: *(cutting in)* Dino! Why d'you 'ave to be so 'orribly *formal*. You
sound so distant. I'm your own darlin'. Minkie, ain't I?

KENNETH: Of course. Yes. I'm.... sorry. Darlin.... Minkie... Just to clear
up the pasties issue, there *was* mustard on them, so that needn't lay on your
conscience. An' I'll eat it all up, if you want me to, but don't jaw me 'bout
diet 'cos you're mixin' me up fritefly. I don't care a damn wot they does in
Berlin thank God I'm British!

(Increasingly comfortable with the 'baby-talk' now)

Wish you was laid up 'ere wiv me. The chambermaid had on a white gown
wiv pink spots this mornin', wot 'stood out' wiv starch an' virtue. P'raps if
you starched your gowns, you wouldn't keep talkin' 'bout spendin' all night
wiv Dino! But p'raps you'd better not starch 'em!

ELSPETH: Minkie can only spend all night wiv Dino, when Dino has asked
Papa...

KENNETH: I play at your bein' 'ere, honeymoonin' and call it our poppy-
moon, cos it's a dream moon. I only 'ope the real one'll be as nice. Come and
be stroked, my sweet, before poppies is quite over.

ELSPETH: The real one'll be twice as nice, and we'll be in Poppyland for
ever, but Dino must write to Papa... Oh London is 'orrid. Stuffy an' 'ot. I'm
worked to death! Luncheons, visits, soirees. Papa is inexhaustible.

KENNETH: Poor Minkie! An' when it's all over you can't go out and play
wiv boats in a harbour like what I can.

ELSPETH: Dino! It's very naughty to waste all your precious strenf messin'
about in boats. I fink boats is your real love.

KENNETH: Minkie darlin', you mustn't fink I'd ever frow you over for boats. Though some is bright blue and some sealin' wax red, which makes 'em hard to resist.

ELSPETH: I fink you don't care nuffin for Minkie slavin' away in stuffy old London with grumpy Papa when all the time 'er heart is in Cornwall with 'er Dino...

KENNETH: But I do care. I've written to your father today.

(*Lighting change. Enter BADGER as PAPA, with a letter*)

ELSPETH: You wished to see me, Papa?

PAPA: Now about this letter.

ELSPETH: What letter?

PAPA: From Kenneth, of course. The answer is no. Over my dead body.

ELSPETH: Don't shout, Papa.

PAPA: (*loudly*) I am not shouting! But I will shout as loudly as is necessary to convey my total opposition to this match. Kenneth may be a good enough fellow, but you scarcely know him.

ELSPETH: What you really mean is that you are afraid of losing your unpaid housekeeper.

PAPA: Arrant nonsense. But since you mention it, who will look after this establishment if you go?

ELSPETH: You will have to pay someone. Or marry again.

PAPA: (*going*) The answer is no!

(*Exit PAPA. Lighting change*)

ELSPETH: In which case, my dearest Dino, we have no alternative but to elope.

KENNETH: Elope?

ELSPETH: We'll run away together to Gretna Green! In a post-chaise!

KENNETH: A post-chaise? All the way to Gretna Green? When?

ELSPETH: Don't be so maddeningly practical. In any case I have been working on dear Papa. I think you will be receiving a letter shortly.

KENNETH: What a relief! Am feeling much steadier on pins. Walked down town today to have a look at the church.

ELSPETH: A church! How unromantic. Next you'll be plaguing me with rings and dreary little bridesmaids.

KENNETH: I do think there should be a ring in the business somewhere – to appease the gods, so to speak.

ELSPETH: I will not be petit bourgeois! I will *not* wear a ring!

KENNETH: Wish we could employ an agency for all the details. Better still, wish I could see you to settle things. And then, darlin' Minks, I could talk to you proper 'bout seaweed and boats and love and such fings. Must go as Mr. Q. 'as just called to take me sailin'.

ELSPETH: Mr. Q.? Who's he?

KENNETH: Arthur Quiller-Couch. He's lent me a skiff, so I can explore all on my own, up creeks and backwaters...You'll meet him when you see fit to come down.

ELSPETH: I am not interested in Mr. Q. I want you! I will not be a martyr to tides!

(*Pause*)

KENNETH: Darlin', 'ow'd you like to go on livin' in London, and come away wiv me for week-ends? Then you needn't write no notes, and it would be so nice and immoral...

ELSPETH: Dino! The idea! I've just been tellin' my aunt how profoundly I love you.

KENNETH: So glad you've told your aunt, 'cos don't think you ever mentioned it to me. As the 22nd is so near, I suppose I may infer the date is fixed for then. Please tell me if the 22nd is absolutely settled, then I can go ahead.

ELSPETH: Absolutely settled. Fings is v.busy but I'll try to get down 2 or 3 days before.

KENNETH: 2 or 3 days! Minkie, I fink you're wrong. An' I fink you will fink you're wrong later.

ELSPETH: I'm busy shoppin'! Shoppin' for clothes! I've found a gorgeous bridal gown – wickedly expensive.

KENNETH: But darlin' two days to go a courtin' is a poor allowance! Dino wants you badly, and at once!

ELSPETH: But soon it'll be next week!

KENNETH: Then it'll be this week! And then what larks, eh?

ELSPETH: What larks!

KENNETH: We'll fink of nuffin' 'cept you and me...

ELSPETH: We'll paddle in pools left by the tide...

KENNETH: I'll hold you all over

ELSPETH: We'll spend all night togevver...

KENNETH: I'll kiss every section of you...

ELSPETH: All night!

KENNETH: An' don't sorst yourself, 'cos I wants to do the sorstin' of you when you gets 'ere - so you've got to save up for your lover, 'oos waitin' for you and is your own lovin'...

ELSPETH: Dino! (*She stands, arms outstretched*)

KENNETH: Minkie! (*He stands, arms outstretched*)

(*Wedding March. ELSPETH and KENNETH rush into each other's arms. Enter RAT, BADGER and TOAD as wedding guests*)

RAT: Congratulations!

BADGER: Well done, old man!

TOAD: Speech! Speech!

(*RAT goes to the piano. KENNETH steps forward*)
(*WEDDING SONG: to the tune of "Early One Morning" [Trad.]*)

KENNETH: Yesterday morning
                  I saw my bride arriving
                  With dress-makers' boxes and a lady's maid in tow
                  Gorgeous her gown and veil

RAT, BADGER, TOAD:
                  And thereby hangs a tale!

KENNETH: How could you treat a poor bridegroom so?
                  The great day is dawning
                  The cry goes up: she's missing!
                  Her breakfast has congealed and we are searching
                              high and low
                  Can she have run away?

RAT, BADGER, TOAD:
                  What – on her wedding day!

KENNETH: (*to ELSPETH*)
                  How could you grieve a poor bridegroom so?

ELSPETH: (*spoken*)
                  It was such a lovely morning, darling – I just had to go out

for a walk. I wandered up to the castle and out onto the headland. The sea was so blue...so calm...I lay on the springy turf and gazed out at the horizon. The cliff-top was freckled with daisies. I made a daisy-chain. Time seemed to stand still...

(*A few bars of "Here comes the Bride" on the piano, and then KENNETH continues with his song*)

KENNETH: The bride is arriving!
The Church is full to bursting
And then behold the spectacle that gave me such a shock!
No wedding gown or train

RAT, BADGER, TOAD:
Sporting a daisy chain!

ALL: Strolling to the altar in a faded cotton frock!

(*End of song. Loud peeling of church bells. RAT, BADGER and TOAD exit with shouts of "Bravo!" "Congratulations!" "Good Luck!" etc. For a moment KENNETH and ELSPETH kiss passionately. Then the bells stop suddenly. Silence. KENNETH disentangles himself.*)

ELSPETH: What's the matter?

(*KENNETH crosses to the arm-chair and sits down*)

ELSPETH: (*going to him*) Dino, what's the matter?

KENNETH: Nothing.

ELSPETH: (*kneeling beside him*) Kiss me again.

(*KENNETH starts to fill a pipe*)

Two boats sharing the same wave. That's us. That's what you wrote. Oh Dino, we don't need no love-post now! We don't need nuffin' 'cept you and me.... haven't you got a kiss for your little Minkie?

KENNETH: (*kindly*) I'm trying to light my pipe.

ELSPETH: You and your pipe...... You're not cross with me, are you?

KENNETH: What for?

ELSPETH: Not wearing my wedding dress.

KENNETH: It was rather singular ... But heavens no.

ELSPETH: Then what is it?

KENNETH: Later perhaps.

ELSPETH: Later! It's the first time we've been alone together for days. Sailing with Q.! Rowing with Q! Night fishing! I married a man, not a yacht club.

KENNETH: Stay in the hotel, if you'd prefer.

ELSPETH: I have no intention of staying in the hotel. I wish to be with my husband. This is our poppy-moon, remember! Night fishing is all very well, but there are other things to do at night.....Aren't there? ... (*She takes his hand*) Dino... Sorst me...

KENNETH: (*attending to his pipe*) I'm busy.

ELSPETH: Busy?　　.

KENNETH: I've got things to do.

ELSPETH: Nonsense. What things?

KENNETH: (*vaguely*) Things.

ELSPETH: We'll share them

KENNETH: You can't share a dream. Dreams are private. (*Smiling*) Keep out.

ELSPETH: You're busy – dreaming! This is absurd!

KENNETH: Oh dreams are very important.

ELSPETH: More important than people?

KENNETH: They're more dependable, certainly.

ELSPETH: Dreams? Dependable?

KENNETH: Oh yes. I learned that when I was very young. They're the gateway to a far better world than this. A world not of tawdry facts and frequent disappointments, but of ideals – the true reality.

ELSPETH: I'm real. I need you, Dino.

(*KENNETH doesn't respond*)

Dino... was it....such a disappointment... the other night?

KENNETH: Oh no. Of course not.

ELSPETH: Then why are you behaving like this?

KENNETH: (*after a moment*) Forgive me, it's only my beastly virtue.

ELSPETH: Virtue? What's that got to do with it?

KENNETH: It's been my enemy all along.

ELSPETH: What on earth are you talking about?

KENNETH: Well, I find it difficult to be.... frankly depraved.

ELSPETH: Depraved? But we're married! I'm not asking you to be depraved, I'm asking you to love me. As you promised.

(*The stage suddenly darkens. Wind and snow effect. KENNETH, now MOLE again, huddles up against the cold and shelters in a 'hollow' in a corner of the stage.*)

RAT'S VOICE: Moly! Moly!

(*RAT enters with a lantern*)

RAT: (*calling*) Moly! Where are you?

MOLE: (*feebly*) Ratty! Is that really you?

RAT: It's me - it's old Rat.

(*RAT joins MOLE in the 'hollow'*)

MOLE: Oh Ratty, I've been so frightened you can't think.

RAT: Oh I quite understand. But you shouldn't really have gone and done it, Mole. I did my best to keep you from it. We river-bankers hardly ever come into the Wild Wood by ourselves. We come in pairs, at least.

MOLE: Sorry, Ratty.

RAT: I think you'd better come and stop with me for a little while. It's very plain and rough, you know – but I can make you comfortable.

MOLE: Oh thank you Ratty. I will!

RAT: Now then we really must pull ourselves together and make a start for home while there's still a little light left. It will never do to spend the night here.

MOLE: Oh no. Of course not.

RAT: Follow me then.

(*Exit RAT. Before MOLE can follow him, the wind and snow effects stop abruptly. Daylight again, but a different lighting state because time has elapsed. MOLE is now KENNETH again.*)

ELSPETH: Where are you off to?

KENNETH: I just thought I'd step round and see G.R.

ELSPETH: What again?

KENNETH: He's finished a painting. He'd like my opinion.

ELSPETH: He's awfully prolific, isn't he?

KENNETH: Yes he is as a matter of fact.

(*Beat*)

ELSPETH: I thought you'd got work to do for the Bank.

KENNETH: Oh,that can wait. There's no urgency for that.

ELSPETH: Shall I expect you for dinner?

KENNETH: Perhaps not.

ELSPETH: And I'd better not wait up.

KENNETH: As you wish.

ELSPETH: Well, let's hope it's another masterpiece.

KENNETH: Goodbye.

(*Exit KENNETH. Lighting change. Sound of "You Made Me Love You" distant, minor key. ELSPETH shivers, puts her cardigan round her shoulders and sits.*)

ELSPETH: (*to herself*) "Goodbye". Always "goodbye". Your favourite word. "Goodbye, I'm going out." "Goodbye, I'm staying in." "Goodbye, I shall be away for a few days... weeks.... months..." "Goodbye, I am locked in a private world, kindly do not disturb." In Cornwall it was Q. In London it was G.R. Always some friend who was more interesting than me. (*Pause*) I was a widow from the very beginning. All those years ago. It was a miracle I became pregnant.

(*Blaze of light and music, as for a 'star' entrance. Enter TOAD*)

TOAD: Poet, playwright, scholar, wit: how many of us achieve a single one of these goals? And for the lucky few it takes a lifetime. This child achieved them all before he was 10 years old. A big welcome for the Jolly Genius! The Fabulous Firstborn! The one and only – ME!

(*TOAD throws open his motoring cape to reveal a child's smock.*)

ELSPETH: (*throwing off her cardigan – rising*) It's a boy! It's a boy!

KENNETH: (*entering*) It's early.

ELSPETH: (*correcting him*) Premature.

(*ELSPETH and KENNETH remove TOAD's cape, cap, goggles etc. He is now ALASTAIR GRAHAME*)

TOAD/ALASTAIR: You two didn't waste much time, did you? Nine and a half months after the wedding. Quick work, eh?

ELSPETH: He's beautiful! Beautiful!

KENNETH: It squints.

ELSPETH: All babies squint.

(*KENNETH takes cape etc. off-stage*)

ELSPETH: So there you are! My little Mouse!

ALASTAIR: I thought my name was Alastair.

ELSPETH: You're my little Mouse, and always will be,

(*She gives him a hug*)

ALASTAIR: Don't. I cannot abide being kissed.

KENNETH: Quite right. Men don't kiss.

ELSPETH: (*to KENNETH*) *Men* do, but not children, like you. You're the child, not he.

KENNETH: As a matter of fact, Mouse, your mother's right. I don't feel at all grown-up. Do you know I can remember everything I felt between the ages of 4 and 7? Nothing has been quite so vivid since.

ELSPETH: Arrested development! Come with me, Mouse. (*Taking him by the hand*) I've got a secret for you.

ALASTAIR: I love secrets.

(*They sit together on the chaise. KENNETH returns to the armchair*)

ELSPETH: (*conspiratorially*) I've had a reply from Mrs. Hardy.

ALASTAIR: Who?

ELSPETH: Mrs.Hardy. She's the wife of Thomas Hardy, who is a very famous author.

ALASTAIR: Like Daddy?

ELSPETH: Oh much more famous than him. I wrote to ask her advice and she says that love - proper and enduring – is not in the nature of men. The most they're capable of is a sort of easy affection – like children.

KENNETH: Mouse! (*ALASTAIR turns*) Would you like to come upstairs and play with my toys?

ALASTAIR: (*eagerly going to him*) Toys?

KENNETH: I've got a whole roomful.

ELSPETH: Mouse!

KENNETH: There's a fish, and a snake, and a beetle that flaps his wings.

They all wind up.

ELSPETH: Mouse! Come *here*!

(*ALASTAIR turns*)

KENNETH: Shall we have a race?

(*ALASTAIR is stranded between them*)

ELSPETH: (*wooingly*) I've got something very exciting to tell you.

ALASTAIR: (*going to her*) Is it a treat?

ELSPETH: *Mr* Hardy likes my poems.

ALASTAIR: What poems?

ELSPETH: My poems, darling. The poems I write. He says they are "charming and remarkable."

KENNETH: I've got a lovely lot of dolls.

ALASTAIR: (*turning*) Dolls?

KENNETH: A whole drawerful.

ALASTAIR: Dolls are soppy.

ELSPETH: Mr. Hardy specially likes my latest poem, which I've simply called "Rejected".

KENNETH: Which reminds me, has anyone been looking after them while I was away?

ELSPETH: (*to herself*) Rejected.

KENNETH: (*to himself*) Dolls need water, seed and groundsel. Or they die.

(*Sudden lighting change. ELSPETH and KENNETH 'freeze'. ALASTAIR lies down slowly centre-stage*)

ELSPETH: (*sharply*) Mouse! What are you doing?

KENNETH: (*relaxed*) Get up out of the road, there's a good fellow.

ELSPETH: Where's Nanny? She should be here!

KENNETH: You'll make yourself all dirty.

(*Sound of approaching motor-car and horn*)

ELSPETH: (*rising*) Look out, there's a motor-car!

ALASTAIR: (*Toad-like*) The motor-car went poop-poop-poop! As it raced along the road.

KENNETH: Get up, you silly boy!

ELSPETH: (*panicking*) Get up! Get up! You'll be killed!

ALASTAIR: Who was it steered it into a pond?

(*Screech of brakes. ALASTAIR rolls nonchalantly aside*)

ALASTAIR: Ingenious Mr. Toad!

(*Lights as before. ALASTAIR leaps up*)

ALASTAIR: (*bowing furiously*) Poop-poop! Poop-poop!Poop-poop!

ELSPETH: (*sitting down*) That was silly and dangerous...

KENNETH: Especially with eyes like yours.

ELSPETH: What *are* you talking about?

KENNETH: His eyes.

ELSPETH: There is nothing whatsoever wrong with his eyes.

KENNETH: The boy is semi-blind, Elspeth. It's a fact we have to face.

ELSPETH: Come here, Mouse. (*Gazing into his eyes*) They're like jewels. They shine as you are going to shine one day. Brilliantly.

ALASTAIR: I shall make pots of money when I grow up.

ELSPETH: Of course you will. You'll be a great man.

ALASTAIR: And when I'm a multi-millionaire, I will stand you a sixpenny ice.

ELSPETH: (*amused*) My darling! Now listen. Have you written any more plays?

ALASTAIR: No.

ELSPETH: Why not?

ALASTAIR: I can't think of anything to write about.

ELSPETH: You're as bad as your father. Still I forgive you. The last one was *so good*. You know I promised to send it to an expert for his opinion? Well... (*She opens drawer in table beside her and produces a letter, which she hands to him*) Read that!

(*ALASTAIR peers at it, holding it close to his face*)

ELSPETH: Quite complimentary, eh?

ALASTAIR: "The sound dramatic..." I can't.

ELSPETH: What?

ALASTAIR: Read it.

ELSPETH: (*taking it from him*) Some of the words are awfully long.

ALASTAIR: It's not that. I can't see properly.

ELSPETH: This is the sentence I like. "The sound dramatic construction resembles Maeterlinck." Maeterlinck!

ALASTAIR: Who's he?

ELSPETH: A very famous author! Will you do it again for me? And play all the parts?

ALASTAIR: Not all. You'll have to help.

ELSPETH: Of course.

ALASTAIR: And I'll rope in old 'Inferiority' as well.

ELSPETH: Mouse! You shouldn't call your father that.

ALASTAIR: You started it. (*Goes to KENNETH, who is snoozing*) Wakey-wakey! I'm doing my play-ay!

KENNETH: What again?

ALASTAIR: You're in it.

KENNETH: Oh, right.

ALASTAIR: (*like a trumpet*) Bah!-baba-bah! Bah! Bah! Mouse Enterprises present: "Scenes from a Short Life".

ELSPETH: What?

ALASTAIR: An Original Play in Three Acts by A. Grahame – aged six and a half.

ELSPETH: You've changed the title.

ALASTAIR: Oh this is a different play. I'm improvising.

ELSPETH: Well stand up straight. You'll never be a proper actor if you slouch.

ALASTAIR: The play explores the picaresque adventures...

ELSPETH: Picaresque! That's a long word.

ALASTAIR: Will you not interrupt! Of a young man named Alastair, known affectionately to family and friends as Mouse. The role of Mouse will be played at this and every performance by – the Author!

ELSPETH: (*applauding*) Bravo!

(*ALASTAIR strides to the picnic hamper. Takes out a bonnet, a bib and a rattle*)

ALASTAIR: Act One. Send for the Doctor.

(*Putting on bib and bonnet*) The year is 1904. The Wright brothers have conquered flight. The speed limit for motor-cars has reached an amazing poop-poop -20 miles per hour. And your intrepid hero has grown too old for such childish pursuits as lying in the path of oncoming vehicles. He is indeed four and a half years old. Mater is in Woodhall Spa, having a nervy turn. Pater is in Spain with one of his boating pals. (*Mock tearful*) And I'm in boring old Broadstairs, boo-hoo, all on my owny-wony. Except for Nanny. I know, I'll get peritonitis. That'll bring 'em running.

(*ALASTAIR sinks to the floor, groaning and writhing in a stylized way*)

(*Collage sound effect of ship's hooter, train whistle, motor-car, running footsteps*)

ELSPETH: (*goes to left of him*) Darling Mouse! I came by the first train..

ALASTAIR: Hello, Mater. (*He resumes writhing*) Aagh! Ooh! Ouch!

KENNETH: (*goes to right of him*) My dear boy! I came by the first boat.

ALASTAIR: Hello, Pater. Aagh! Ooh! Ouch!

ELSPETH: Quick! Summon the surgeon!

KENNETH: Righty-ho. (*He sits in the armchair and starts work on the crossword*)

ELSPETH: (*to ALASTAIR, bending down to him*) Darling how *are* you?

ALASTAIR: It still hurts.

ELSPETH: You're so *brave*. I really must sit down.

(*ELSPETH goes to chaise*)

ALASTAIR: (*no longer stylized*) You've been away for ages. You might at least have written.

ELSPETH: I was too ill to write letters, Mouse. My doctor specifically forbade it. In fact, I cut short my convalescence to come and see you.

ALASTAIR: I'm sorry to be a nuisance.

ELSPETH: You're not! My precious! The doctor insisted that I rest my nerves completely. Just sit on the sofa all day and sip hot water.

ALASTAIR: (*to KENNETH*) Can I have a story?

KENNETH: (*interested again*) Of course you can. Now where were we?

ALASTAIR: You've been away so long I've forgotten.

KENNETH: Ah yes. The shy little Mole had just left his home – in the middle of spring cleaning, as far as I remember. It was a perfect spring day. The hedgerows were singing in the mellow sunshine. At last he reached the river bank. The Mole had never seen a river before. It glided by, dark and mysterious. He peered into a hole in the bank and what should he see but some whiskers and above the whiskers two round little eyes gleaming out at him. It was the...

(*Enter RAT as DOCTOR in formal clothes with a doctor's bag*)

DOCTOR: Well, I'm happy to say that the operation was a complete success. The wound is healing nicely.

ELSPETH: Brave as a lion.

DOCTOR: Hello, young man. How are you feeling today?

(*Pause*)

KENNETH: Come on, Mouse. Say 'hello' to the doctor.

ALASTAIR: Hello, doctor, are your bowels open today?

(*ELSPETH laughs*)

KENNETH: Mouse! That's not a very nice thing to say.

ALASTAIR: Not nice? Then why is he always saying it to me? I didn't start it, he said it first. (*Chanting*) Are your bowels open today-ay-ay? (*He shakes his rattle*) Are your bowels open today-ay-ay?

ELSPETH: Plainsong! At the age of 4!

DOCTOR: Have you no control over your offspring?

KENNETH: Not much.

ALASTAIR: Well are they open or not?

DOCTOR: Really!

ALASTAIR: I expect they're closed for lunch!

DOCTOR: Disgraceful behaviour!

(*KENNETH hustles the DOCTOR out; ALASTAIR bows furiously*)

ELSPETH: (*applauding*) Well acted, Mouse. That was hilarious. You've quite cheered me up

ALASTAIR: (*sweeping on*) Act Two. The Lonely Young Man.

ELSPETH: Lonely? You were never lonely. You were always a social animal.

(*ALASTAIR is at the hamper. He has taken off his bonnet and bib and has put on a large white sun-hat and carries a small child's spade.*)

(*RAT - no longer the DOCTOR –re-enters and goes to the piano*)

ALASTAIR: Littlehampton! The seaside!

(*SONG: 'I Do Like To Be Beside The Seaside'. [Music: John Glover-Kind]*)

> Oh I do like to be beside the seaside,
> I do like to be beside the sea,
> I do like to stroll along the prom-prom-prom,
> Where the brass band plays tiddley-om-pom-pom!
> Oh I do like to be beside the seaside,
> I'd be beside myself with glee;
> *But* I'm 'ere all on me own
> With me Nanny far from 'ome -
> Me Ma and Pa *'ave* deserted me!

ELSPETH: (*spoken*) Nonsense. We had to stay at home for your father's work. If you're going to be silly, I shan't listen.

(*She picks up a photograph album*)

ALASTAIR:

> (*sings*)
> They've bin and gone to 'orrid Cornwall
> 'Cos Littlehampton's not their cup of tea –
> Oh I'd raise a hearty cheer
> If only they was 'ere
> Beside me beside the sea.

(*RAT exits. ALASTAIR is on his knees now, 'digging' in a desultory fashion. In the following section each character is in a separate pool of light and plays out front*)

ELSPETH: (*leafing through album*) What he sees in Littlehampton I cannot imagine. A horrid little place, simply swarming with the wrong people.

KENNETH: Greenbank Hotel, Falmouth, Cornwall. My darling Mouse. This is a birthday letter to wish you many happy returns of the day. Seven! What an age! I wish our taste in places was similar, so that we could be together.

ALASTAIR: So do I. Birthdays aren't so chirpy with only Nanny.

KENNETH: But we will meet again soon, and then we will have *treats*.

(*ALASTAIR produces paper and pencil from a pocket of his smock and lies on the floor, eyes very close to the paper.*)

ALASTAIR: (*as he writes*) Dear Dad. How soon is soon? Could you come here for the weekend? Please do.

KENNETH: I have sent you two picture- books: one about Brer Rabbit from Daddy; and one about some other animals, from Mummy. And we have sent you a boat, painted red, with mast and sail, to sail in the round pond by the windmill.

(*ALASTAIR crosses out 'Dad' and writes 'Mum'*)

ALASTAIR: Dear Mum, can't you come for the weekend? Please do. I miss you very much.

KENNETH: And Mummy has sent you a boat-hook to catch the boat when it comes ashore. Also Mummy has sent you some sand-toys to play in the sand with, and a card game.

ALASTAIR: (*crosses out 'Mum' and writes 'Both'*) Dear Both. How dare you not come here for the weekend. I like it so much at Littlehampton that I want to live here. Yours, A.Grahame.

(*ALASTAIR screws up the paper and throws it off-stage*)

KENNETH: Have you heard about the Toad?

ALASTAIR: Course I have, silly. D'you think I'd forget my favourite character, and all those exciting stories you told me to help me go to sleep. Wish you were here now. It's not the same when Nanny reads it. A bed-time story by post – I ask you! (*Sitting up*) I shall change my name. I shall change my name to Robinson. Michael Robinson. It's a far finer name than – ugh - Alastair Grahame.

(*He stands up and bows. Luke-warm applause from ELSPETH and KENNETH*)

ALASTAIR: Act Three. Enter Robinson! There will now be a short pause while I change my props.

(*Lighting change. ALASTAIR goes to the hamper and takes off his hat and child's smock, revealing 'prep' school jersey and short trousers. Takes out a scroll and a toy revolver*)

ELSPETH: (*turning to KENNETH*) Robinson... Wasn't that the name of the lunatic?

KENNETH: What lunatic?

ELSPETH: He came into the Bank and fired a revolver at you.

KENNETH: Oh that. It was a long time ago.

ALASTAIR: (*waving toy revolver, scroll stuck in his belt*) I am Robinson!

And I wish to see the Secretary of the Bank of England!

ELSPETH: You must remember. He tried to kill you.

ALASTAIR: (*firing toy revolver*) Bang! Bang!

KENNETH: Luckily he missed.

ALASTAIR: (*producing scroll*) Read this! Or I'll blow your brains out!

ELSPETH: That's right! He produced a scroll or something and kept waving it at you.

ALASTAIR: Read it!

KENNETH: (*kindly*) It looks awfully long, Mouse.

ALASTAIR: READ IT!

KENNETH: Very well. (*Takes the scroll*)

ALASTAIR: Aha! That proves it. Guilty!

KENNETH: What is all this?

ALASTAIR: (*the prosecuting counsel*) Examine the scroll closely and you will note that it is tied at either end with a ribbon: one white, one black. I offered you the scroll lengthwise. It was open to you to grasp either end. (*Momentously*) And you chose the end bound by the black ribbon. Guilty!

ELSPETH: What a memory the boy has! He's remembered every detail.

ALASTAIR: (*taking the scroll from KENNETH*) I shall now read the charges.

KENNETH: Do we have to continue with this charade?

ELSPETH: I think it's rather fun.

ALASTAIR: (*who has untied the ribbons and unrolled the scroll*) Dear Sir!

ELSPETH: He was never as polite as that.

ALASTAIR: (*rounding on ELSPETH*) And Madam!

ELSPETH: Madam who?

ALASTAIR: You!

ELSPETH: Me? It has nothing to do with me.

ALASTAIR: Oh yes it has.

ELSPETH: I wasn't there.

ALASTAIR: Exactly! (*Reading from scroll*) Dear Sir and Madam! One. Why didn't you come and see me in my school play?

ELSPETH: That has nothing to do with the lunatic.

ALASTAIR: No, but it has a lot to do with me.

ELSPETH: In any case, last time you forgot your lines.

ALASTAIR: I know I did, but it was only an amateur performance, with *very* amateur actors. Not up to the standard of Sarah Bernhardt and Sir Henry Irving, I know. But it was very exciting for me as I was actually in it.

ELSPETH: Mouse, we would have come, we *wanted* to come....

ALASTAIR: Then why didn't you?

ELSPETH: There were simply no trains.

ALASTAIR: No trains?

ELSPETH: Were there, Kenneth?

KENNETH: (*yawning*) Don't expect so.

ALASTAIR: I thought you were keen on plays.

ELSPETH: We prefer it if you write them

ALASTAIR: (*reading from the scroll*) Two. Why couldn't I come home for the Coronation? Everyone else did, except the boys whose parents live in Timbuktoo or somewhere. And Three. Do you know the date of the end of term?

ELSPETH: Don't be silly, darling.

ALASTAIR: I keep telling you and you keep forgetting.

ELSPETH: Well, it's ...Thursday week, isn't it?

ALASTAIR: *No*, it's *Tuesday*! Tuesday December the 19th, in the year of our Lord, 1911, is that clear? I do *not* wish to be left at school for Christmas!

ELSPETH: (*after a slight pause*) I'm getting awfully tired of your little plays.

ALASTAIR: (*sadly*) Varium et mutabile semper est femina.

ELSPETH: (*brightening*) The Latin's coming on!

(*Pause. KENNETH returns to his crossword. ELSPETH puts away the photograph album. ALASTAIR looks deflated – the end of an unsuccessful performance.*)

ALASTAIR: Wish I could have Jack to stay. Please can I? He's my pal.

ELSPETH: Mouse, you'll make me ill! For the umpteenth time that subject is closed.

ALASTAIR: I shall run away to the stage, and take Jack with me, if he'll come.

ELSPETH: You'll do nothing of the kind. You'll clear away your junk and go to bed.

ALASTAIR: Anyway I don't care. I've got one pal who's with me always. He's the Carpenter.

ELSPETH: A carpenter! I didn't think we knew any carpenters.

ALASTAIR: He's Jesus Christ.

ELSPETH: That fairy-tale! Never mind, you'll grow up one day.

(*Pointing to the scroll*) Don't forget that.

ALASTAIR: (*handing it to ELSPETH*) That's for you.

(*Exit ALASTAIR*)

ELSPETH: For me? I wasn't the guilty one. It belonged to your father, not me. He was the one who had the nightmares. Nightmares that reeked of guilt. (*Examining the scroll*) A white ribbon at one end and a black at the other. And he chose the wrong end. Guilty! Guilty in all departments.

(*Lighting change. Sounds of a wood at night. Spotlight on KENNETH, who is briefly MOLE again*)

KENNETH: They're catching up with me! I must run faster! Faster! I must hide.... I can see a face! An evil wedge-shaped face... and another! - and another! In every hole, every hollow...hundreds of them ... The whole wood is after me! Hunting, chasing, closing in! Ratty! Badger! Save me!

(*Lighting change. Noise of vast banquet. Enter RAT and BADGER as Bank of England officials in evening dress. They place an upright chair centre and stand either side of it*)

OFFICIAL 1: Gentlemen!

(*Noise of banquet stops dead*)

Before I ask you

OFFICIAL 2: To raise your glasses

OFFICIAL 1: And drink the health

OFFICIAL 2: Of our retiring Secretary

OFFICIAL 1: Mr Kenneth Grahame...

KENNETH: What?

OFFICIAL 1: I beg your pardon?

KENNETH: Retiring?

OFFICIAL 1: Of course.

KENNETH: I don't understand.

OFFICIAL 1: (*to OFFICIAL 2*) Have a word with him.

(*OFFICIAL 2 goes over to KENNETH*)

OFFICIAL 2: (*confidentially*) The new Governor recommends your immediate retirement.

KENNETH: But I'm only 49.

OFFICIAL 2: For health reasons.

KENNETH: My health is far from perfect, I know. There have been absences due to illness, but...

OFFICIAL 2: (*as kindly as he can*) You leave the office early, you arrive late, you take exceptionally long holidays. The new Governor will not tolerate passengers.

KENNETH: I must see *something* of my family.

ELSPETH: (*harshly*) What family?

OFFICIAL 1: You have neglected your family.

OFFICIAL 2: Trips abroad with your boating friends.

OFFICIAL 1: "Got to stay in town due to pressure of work."

ELSPETH: You're an absentee father. An absentee husband!

KENNETH: Well, I – I write books...

OFFICIAL 1: What have you produced in the last ten years?

KENNETH: Let me think...let me think...

OFFICIAL 2: Nothing.

KENNETH: Wait. I wrote a short story for my son's nursery magazine. *Bertie's Escapade*. About a pig...who goes carol-singing...

OFFICIAL 2: (*as politely as he can*) How riveting.

OFFICIAL 1: Nothing! Despite being bullied by publishers.

KENNETH: I am a spring, not a pump. Oh and I have a manuscript that I'm hoping will be accepted. Based on some bed-time stories I told my son.

ELSPETH: I was the driving force behind that.

KENNETH: How can you say such a thing? That is simply not true.

ELSPETH: Who preserved the Toad letters?

KENNETH: Nanny did.

ELSPETH: And who dug them out of the drawer when that publishing woman came sniffing around for any scraps you could throw her?

KENNETH: *The Wind in the Reeds* - or whatever I finally call it – owes nothing to you whatsoever.

ELSPETH: Oh! Then to whom does it owe something?

KENNETH: That little book is free from problems.

ELSPETH: Your boating pals? Your painter friend?

KENNETH: Clean of the clash of sex.

ELSPETH: A good thing, too. On that subject you know less than nothing.

KENNETH: It's about life; and fresh air; and open spaces.

OFFICIAL 2: All of which you will shortly be free to indulge to your heart's content. You are requested to retire forthwith.

KENNETH: Couldn't I continue - for a few months or so – at least until my book is published?

OFFICIAL 2: Your pension will be £400 per annum.

ELSPETH: Is that all?

KENNETH: Is that *all*? After 29 years? It should be at least twice that!

OFFICIAL 1: And now, gentlemen, raise your glasses and drink the health of – Mr Grahame.

(*Sound of standing ovation*)

OFFICIALS: Speech! Speech!

KENNETH: I can't. Not in front of all these people.

OFFICIALS: Speech! Speech!

KENNETH: There are hundreds and hundreds of them!

OFFICIALS, ELSPETH: (*insisting*) *Speech*!

(*Sudden silence*)

OFFICIAL 1: Pray silence for Mr. Grahame!

(The lights fade to a single 'spot' above KENNETH, who stands in front of the central chair. A preparatory cough. He clears his throat. Silence. He has 'dried'. He stares out at the audience transfixed.)

ELSPETH: *(quietly)* He can't think of anything to say.

OFFICIAL 1: TURN – HIM – OUT!

(Sound of hubbub. Cries of "Out! Out! Out!" Strobe perhaps...)

ELSPETH: *(cutting through)* No! Wait!

(Lighting change. The hubbub stops as abruptly as it started. KENNETH is sitting on the central chair holding a book)

He did have something to say.

(RAT and BADGER, now as LITERARY CRITICS, are either side of KENNETH. Sound of cocktail party)

CRITIC 1: A book at last!

CRITIC 2: Congratulations, my dear fellow!

CRITIC 1: I'm so pleased for you!

CRITIC 2: After the ten-year gestation!

CRITIC 1: I know "The – er – Wind in the Whatsits" will be a huge success.

CRITIC 2: Despite the somewhat grisly reviews.

CRITIC 1: "A bread-and-butter 'Jungle Book'".

(They laugh)

CRITIC 2: Rather witty, one has to admit.

(THE CRITICS now ignore KENNETH and talk over his head.)

CRITIC 1: Of course in my opinion he should stick to writing about children. I *much* preferred *The Golden Age*.

CRITIC 2: So did I. So did I. Did you know that the Bodley Head turned this one down flat?

CRITIC 1: My dear! Who didn't? Poor Curtis has gone absolutely hairless hawking the thing round.

CRITIC 2: On both sides of the Atlantic.

CRITIC 1: Awfully sporting of Methuen to give it a try.

CRITIC 2: Indeed, indeed. But did you know that he couldn't actually bring himself to guarantee an advance?

(*They laugh*)

ELSPETH: Gentlemen! (*Sweetly*) Did you read Mr Middleton of *Vanity Fair*?

CRITIC 1: Oh Middleton does the Highland Fling about anything.

ELSPETH: Teddy Roosevelt loved it. It's to be published in New York.

CRITIC 2: My dear, in America they do the strangest things.

ELSPETH: And did you see the sales figures?

CRITICS: Can't say we did.

(*She hands a sheet of paper to CRITICS*)

CRITIC 1: My God!

CRITIC 2: Look at this!

CRITIC 1: Second edition already!

CRITIC 2: The damn thing's a best-seller!

ELSPETH: More champagne, gentlemen?

CRITIC 1: Well I always said the book had *something*.

CRITIC 2: So did I, so did I. It was only a matter of time, wasn't it?

CRITIC 1: (*singing*) Fo-or he's a jolly good fellow!

CRITIC 2: (*singing, nudged by CRITIC 1*) For he's a jolly good fellow

BOTH CRITICS: For he's a jolly good fe-e-llow!

ELSPETH: Now he'll write a whole string of masterpieces!

(*to KENNETH*) Won't you, Kenneth?

(*KENNETH looks uncertain, gets up and exits. CRITICS look at each other*)

CRITICS: (*spoken*) And so say all of us.

(*Blackout*)

ACT TWO

(A second later. ELSPETH is the old woman again, alone in her room. The old frayed cardigan is round her shoulders. She is picking at the remains of the chicken drumstick that was her 'breakfast')

ELSPETH: *(singing to herself)*
          We owe it all to Mouse
          We owe it all to Mouse,
          For he's a jolly good fellow!
          We owe it all to Mouse.

(She starts to re-wrap carefully the remains of the chicken, and replace them in the paper bag)

I forgive you, Dino. For all the disappointments. The books you never wrote. The love we never shared. Years of dejection; anger; wrong. After all you gave me Mouse, and he made up for everything. So brilliant; so witty; so understanding. A young St Francis. I can see him now, our first Christmas at Blewbury, standing up to sing a carol in front of the whole village. So tall in the light of the storm-lantern. The rough villagers in the shadows at his feet. He sang as sweetly as an angel.....

(Banging of a tin drum. Blaze of light. Enter ALASTAIR in glasses, long trousers, with a home-made tabard thrown over his everyday clothes and a 'period' hat perched jauntily on his head. He has a toy drum round his neck and is waving a wooden spoon)

ELSPETH: *(throwing off cardigan and wincing)* Don't please! My nerves.

ALASTAIR: *(stamping round the stage – at the top of his voice)*
The Mummers are here, the Mummers are here!

ELSPETH: Mouse! You'll make me ill again.

ALASTAIR: I'm doing a mumming play.

ELSPETH: Can't you 'mum' quietly?

ALASTAIR: Mummers aren't quiet.

ELSPETH: Don't remind me. They were worse than ever this year. What cheap comic songs from the London music halls have to do with good old "St. George and the Dragon" I shall never know.

ALASTAIR: *(beating drum)* Pray silence for the Prologue!

ELSPETH: Very well. If we must.

ALASTAIR: *(Berkshire accent)*
          Here be I, Master Mouse,

To tell a tale to all this house,
A tale o' woe so drab and drear
That you won't 'scape shedding a tear.
Brave St. George....

(*He gestures to the empty arm-chair where KENNETH usually sits*)

Where is he? Where's "Inferiority"?

ELSPETH: Walking – where do you think.

ALASTAIR: And dragon she (*gesturing to ELSPETH*)
Were locked in deadly enmity.
Bur never fear, no blood did flow –
Yet harm was done, as you will see.
The victim? An innocent third partee.

ELSPETH: Whatever are you going on about?

ALASTAIR: I will not tell what is his name, I'll simply say: "It's a great big shame!"

(*Enter RAT, also wearing a jaunty 'Mummers' hat. He sits down at the piano*)

ELSPETH: What is?

ALASTAIR: What?

ELSPETH: A great big shame.

ALASTAIR: Nothing. It's a song.

ELSPETH: Why didn't you say so?

ALASTAIR: A music-hall song!

ELSPETH: How vulgar!

ALASTAIR: It's my favourite!

ELSPETH: You're as bad as the mummers.

(*SONG: 'It's a Great Big Shame'. [Music: George Le Brunn]*)

ALASTAIR: (*speaking to chords, in the cockney style of Gus Elen*)
I've lost my Dad – he's the best in all the land,
But don't you think 'im dead, because 'e ain't.
But since 'e's wed, it's as though 'e's bin unmanned –
It's enough to vex the temper of a saint.
'E wrote *The Wind in the Willows*, but that was thanks to me
And at the Bank 'e soldiered on o'course;
But now that 'e's retired, 'e's as silent as a tree –
Oh I wish as I could get 'im a divorce!

ELSPETH: (*spoken*) Divorce! I don't think that is a subject suitable for a boy of your age.

ALASTAIR: (*singing*)
   It's a great big shame,
   And if she belonged to me,
   I'd really beat the drum;
   Shuttin' up a feller what has won world fame
   And 'er just a measly mum.
   They 'adn't bin married not a month nor more,
   When 'e knows just what a fool 'e's bin;
   Isn't it a pity that the likes of 'er
   Should put upon the likes of 'im.

ELSPETH: (*spoken*) Mouse! You sound so common.

(*Enter KENNETH, dressed in plus-fours, a soft shirt and a baggy tweed coat. He is carrying an ice-cream. He sits in the arm-chair as before, and starts slowly and meticulously to eat the ice-cream*)

ALASTAIR: 'E was like Samson when 'e'd 'ad 'is barnet done.

ELSPETH: Another ice-cream. I hope you realise it's your second today.

KENNETH: It's my third.

ELSPETH: Disgusting. You eat like a pig.

KENNETH: (*between licks*) The pig, my dear Elspeth is a noble creature. Some of my best friends are pigs.

ELSPETH: You prefer pigs to people.

KENNETH: Perhaps they are less demanding.

(*During the following the lights fade, leaving ALASTAIR in a central pool of light*)

ALASTAIR: (*to chords*)
   I'm in the middle;
   I'm the little pig – And what I thinks I never even hint,
   I've a cataract in one eye, but I don't give a fig,
   I got acne and the other 'as a squint;
   But it's 'ard to study when your eyes get tired and sting,
   Yet I passed the Common Entrance – what a brain!
   Dad takes me to the circus – what we call 'The Magic
      Ring';

   Oh I'm not the sort of feller to complain:

(*sings*)
It's a great big shame
And I'd give the other eye
If I could 'ave me say-
Naggin' at a little lad what don't 'arf try
And they getting old and grey –
I 'adn't bin born not a month nor more
When a genius I've got to be;
Isn't it a pity that the likes of them
Should put upon the likes of *me*!

(*Clanging of school bell. Sound of running feet. RAT puts on a school cap and is now a RUGBY SCHOOLBOY*)

BOY: Hurry up, you'll be late!

ALASTAIR: Late? What for?

BOY: Call-over, stupid. You get beaten if you're late for call-over.

ALASTAIR: Beaten? Who by?

BOY: The Sixth.

ALASTAIR: Sixth what?

BOY: Sixth *form*! Wakey! Wakey! – You're at Rugby!

(*Bell again. BOY stands to attention*)

ELSPETH: Come on, Mouse. Enough of this play-acting. Have you finished your packing?

ALASTAIR: No.

ELSPETH: Well hurry up.

(*During the following she removes ALASTAIR'S tabard and hat revealing a Rugby School blazer.*)

ALASTAIR: Wish I was going back to the Malthouse.

KENNETH: That's natural. You were happy there.

ELSPETH: It was a dear little school. But you're a young man now. Isn't that exciting?

(*Puts the school cap on his head*)

ALASTAIR: Mrs. Corbett took us for lovely picnics on the beach.

KENNETH: I'm sure you'll like Rugby.

ALASTAIR: (*wistfully*) I like Mrs. Corbett.

ELSPETH: You did so well at The Malthouse.

ALASTAIR: I won the 'Reading and Recitation' prize. And I learnt to swim! The waves were fierce but I didn't care. I swam over the ledge, out into the open sea...

(*Bell louder*)

BOY: You'll be late.

ALASTAIR: And me and Jennings found this cave in a quarry. We had a ripping game. He was Rupert of Hentzau (*Putting his hands in his pockets and swaggering*) and I was Dick Lawless!

BADGER'S VOICE: (*off-stage, on echo*) Take your hands out of your pockets!

ALASTAIR: (*obeying nonchalantly*) The bloody buchaneer!

(*He whistles boldly*)

BADGER'S VOICE: (*off-stage – on echo*) No whistling in the corridor!

ALASTAIR: (*swaggering*) Fifteen men on a dead man's....

BADGER'S VOICE: (*off-stage – on echo*) STOP LOITERING!

ALASTAIR: (*sighing*) I suppose one is permitted to go to the lavatory. I shall lock myself in.

BOY: You'll have a job. There aren't any doors.

ALASTAIR: (*sitting on the floor*) No doors! Who runs this barbarian establishment?

ELSPETH: (*who's been highly amused by ALASTAIR'S pert answers*) Brilliant! You'll sweep the board at Rugby!

(*ALASTAIR takes a book out of his pocket and starts to read.*
Enter BADGER as a SCHOOL PREFECT)

PREFECT: Right! Answer your names (*Rattling them off- BOY answering 'here' to each name*) Wade, Seymour-Garton, Poole, Innes-Jones, Grahame... Grahame?

(*Silence*)

PREFECT: (*ominously*) What is the number of his dormitory?

(*Blackout. Exit BOY. PREFECT stands over ALASTAIR shining a torch in his face*)

You cut call-over. Why?

ALASTAIR: I was reading a book.

PREFECT: Reading a book, eh? During call-over.

ALASTAIR: It's the only time I can get any peace and quiet.

PREFECT: Show. (*ALASTAIR hands him the book*) *The Bible in Spain* by George Borrow. I see: an airy-fairy blighter. Well, even airy-fairy blighters can't get away with breaking House rules.

ALASTAIR: There are so many.

PREFECT: Tax the old grey cells, do they? You're a bumbler, Grahame. And in this House we don't like bumblers.

ALASTAIR: I may be a bit of a – what you say – but one day I'll be a great man. Mummy says so.

PREFECT: Really? Mummy says that, does she? And what does Daddy say?

ALASTAIR: He hardly opens his mouth as a matter of fact. He's Kenneth Grahame, you know.

PREFECT: Who?

ALASTAIR: *The* Kenneth Grahame. Creator of Toad.

PREFECT: Who?

ALASTAIR: Never heard of Mr. Toad? You are ignorant.

(*ELSPETH chuckles*)

PREFECT: (*turning*) Who's that laughing? (*Back to ALASTAIR, furious*) I'm not ignorant, Grahame, you are. You are the worst fag in the history of this House. You're useless at rugger. Hopeless at Corps – fancy carrying your rifle upside down! Didn't you notice what the others were doing?

ALASTAIR: I was keeping my eyes to the front.

PREFECT: *Silence!* You're in a world of your own, aren't you? Well I intend to beat you into the real one. Beat you till you're black and blue if necessary. Do you understand?

ALASTAIR: Yes.

PREFECT: Now come with me into the study, and we'll see whether you come out the same "Toad" that you went in!

(*Exit PREFECT and ALASTAIR. Sound of ALASTAIR being beaten. ELSPETH, who doesn't wish to remember this, busies herself getting a piece of white sheet out of the drawer in the table beside her. The thwacks mix into the sound of marching feet. ELSPETH starts cutting the sheet into strips for bandages, humming to herself, "It's a Long Way to Tipperary". KENNETH rises from his chair.)*

KENNETH: Platoon, halt!

(Sound of platoon halting, raggedly)

Right turn!

(Sound of platoon doing this but not together)

(He faces the audience and addresses them)

Stand at ease! Stand easy. Thank you, gentlemen. That's a great improvement. A few more weeks and the Blewbury Veterans will be more than a match for the Kaiser. The next parade will be at the same time next week in Mr. Caudwell's barn. Platoon, dis-miss!

(Sound of men dispersing)

ELSPETH: How were they?

KENNETH: Dreadful.

ELSPETH: You shouldn't waste your time with them.

KENNETH: At least we provide entertainment for the barn cat. He sits on the wheatsacks reviewing the troops. He thinks the whole charade is specially got up for his benefit. What *are* you doing?

ELSPETH: Making bandages, can't you see? The field hospitals are crying out for them.

KENNETH: The Veterans have elected me their commanding officer, only because they think I'm the most military looking. Not for any other reason. Takes me back to the London Scottish days.

ELSPETH: Thrilling, isn't it? Mouse starting out at Rugby. Our brave boys in Flanders rescuing poor little Belgium. The world is suddenly young again!

KENNETH: Meanwhile we really should try and solve the servant problem.

ELSPETH: No time to worry about that.

KENNETH: But the garden's going to pot, and the house is filthy. Do you realise there are mice nesting in the larder?

ELSPETH: We're at war, Kenneth. At a time when our entire civilisation is threatened by the forces of evil and barbarism, we cannot be distracted by the unscheduled arrival of a few small rodents.

(She replaces the remaining sheet and bandages in the drawer and takes out a strange-looking garment. She holds it up against KENNETH, measuring it for size.)

KENNETH: I must confess that one's patriotism falters when the servants join up.

ELSPETH: It's your fault. You're on the recruiting committee.

KENNETH: (*reacting to the garment*) What on earth is it?

ELSPETH: The new underwear. (*She pins it up round him*) Special thermal underwear. You wear it and wear it. Saves all that endless washing.

KENNETH: Is it hygienic?

ELSPETH: Oh yes. You change it every year.

(*Returns to chaise and sits down*) I'll just sew this up, and then I must go hunting while the light holds. If only we didn't have to eat.

KENNETH: (*remaining standing*) I wish you wouldn't.

ELSPETH: Wouldn't what?

KENNETH: Go... hunting, as you call it.

ELSPETH: We haven't a thing for supper.

KENNETH: You make yourself such a spectacle, clattering down the village street chasing after stray chickens.

ELSPETH: I only hunt the dead ones, dear: I'm not as young as I was.

(*Lighting change. ELSPETH continues sewing. KENNETH goes to the writing desk, sits down and takes out pen and paper.*)

Don't tell me you're going to write something at last.

(*Conspiratorial*) What's it to be?

KENNETH: (*writing*) Dear Purves,

ELSPETH: A letter to that American professor. How disappointing! And there was I positively drooling at the prospect of another masterpiece.

(*Lights fade to a single spot on KENNETH*)

KENNETH: I'm wracking my brains trying to find a good excuse for not having written to you. Overwork? I'm retired. The social whirl? I rarely see anyone. In fact I hardly get out at all now, as we are surrounded by a sea of mud. I never knew mud was so potent. And gale after gale comes battering down on us...Yet, do you know, I do write you any quantity of magnificent letters. In my armchair of evenings, with closed eyes. Strolling in the woods or on the downs. Or with head on pillow, late, on a thoroughly wet and disagreeable morning. I see my pen covering page after page. I feel myself lick the envelope. I see myself running to the post. I hear the flop of the letter in the box...

(*Lights up on ELSPETH with a brown envelope*)

ELSPETH: It's not a letter, it's a telegram.

KENNETH: It's all so real to me, that I was quite surprised that you weren't asking me to limit them to, say three a week.

ELSPETH: (*starting to open the envelope*) Must be a mistake; we've got noone at the Front.

KENNETH: Such good stuff too - witty, anecdotal, pensive, pathetic...

ALASTAIR'S VOICE: (*off-stage-amplified*) This is an S.O.S. Please take me away from this school.

ELSPETH: (*staring at the telegram*) But it's only a few days till half-term.

ALASTAIR'S VOICE: I can't wait till half-term. I want to come home. Now.

(*Pause*)

(*ELSPETH sits staring at the telegram. ALASTAIR enters in Rugby School blazer and cap, carrying 2 large suitcases*)

KENNETH: (*jumping up*) Mouse, how are you? Allow me.

(*He takes the suitcases from ALASTAIR and places them at the side of the stage*)

KENNETH: (*returning to his armchair*) Well ...aren't you going to take your cap off?

ALASTAIR: (*to ELSPETH*) Aren't you going to say "Hello"?

ELSPETH: (*putting down the telegram*) Mouse, darling, how are you? Come and tell me all about it.

(*She beckons him to sit beside her. He goes to her but remains standing*)

My poor lamb, what did they do to you?

(*ALASTAIR says nothing*)

KENNETH: Try to talk to us, Mouse. Tell us what went wrong.

(*ALASTAIR says nothing*)

ELSPETH: Don't be brave. Tell us.

KENNETH: I'm surprised you didn't get on with the other boys, Mouse.

ALASTAIR: How can one talk to people whose only powers of conversation lie in their elbows?

ELSPETH: Never mind. You have a good rest and you'll go back quite refreshed.

ALASTAIR: I'm not going back.

ELSPETH: Of course you are.

ALASTAIR: I am not going back.

ELSPETH: You can't simply give up. This is only your first term. Besides Rugby is one of the best schools in the country.

ALASTAIR: It's not. It's the worst.

ELSPETH: How can you say such a thing?

ALASTAIR: It's horrible. Horrible.

ELSPETH: Now you're being ridiculous.

KENNETH: What made it so horrible, Mouse? Was it just the other boys?

ALASTAIR: (*after a pause*) Everything. The boys...the food...the work.... the games...the stupid rules...the masters..... everything.

ELSPETH: I thought you liked the masters.

ALASTAIR: Only "Roger Rum". He said I could go and sit in his dining-room whenever I felt unhappy. But you can't be there all the time, and you always have the awful thought of going back.

KENNETH: Weren't things better after I'd arranged for you to change studies?

ALASTAIR: A bit. My new study-mate at least tolerated me. But the studies are so small – like prison cells – to be cooped up with anyone is dreadful. I wish I was good at rugger. If you're good at rugger you're a useful member of the House and the boys like you. They don't mind if your fagging is inefficient. They don't mind if you forget all those endless stupid rules. But if you're a bumbler, they beat you. And they go on beating you till you remember. But I don't think I ever will – because they're *pointless*. The whole place is pointless. Please! Don't make me go back! Ever!

(*Exit ALASTAIR*)

(*Pause*)

KENNETH: We'd better take soundings about another school.

ELSPETH: Six weeks! It was hardly worth buying the uniform!

KENNETH: If not Rugby, where?

ELSPETH: It's such a terrible admission of failure.

KENNETH: I'll go and see Quiller-Couch. (*He rises*)

ELSPETH: Your boating pal. What does he know about schools?

KENNETH: As a professor at Cambridge, a fair amount, I imagine.

(*Lighting change. KENNETH knocks on an imaginary door. Sound effect off-stage*)

ELSPETH: I don't trust Mr. Q.

KENNETH: *Sir* Q.

ELSPETH: I hold him responsible for ruining our honeymoon. Dragging you away on endless yachting trips.

KENNETH: You were invited.

(*He knocks again*)

ELSPETH: (*strident*) I did not anticipate a honeymoon a trois!

Q'S VOICE: (*off-stage-vehement*) God! God! Is there no peace in this blasted college?

(*RAT as 'Q" emerges in stockinged feet, wearing a silk dressing gown*)

Q: Rappers, you're early...(*sees KENNETH*) Kenneth, my dear fellow! (*They shake hands*) I do apologise. I thought you were Rappers.

KENNETH: Rappers?

Q: E.J.Rapson, Professor of Sanskrit. Come in old fellow. Sit down.

KENNETH: You're changing. I'll come back in a few minutes,.

Q: No you won't. Sit down. Frightful bore changing. Spot of company cheers one up. Sorry to hear about the boy.

(*Exit Q. KENNETH sits on an upright chair. Almost at once Q returns in shirt-tails, with a white bow-tie about his neck. He is carrying the rest of his evening dress:trousers, white waist-coat and tailcoat. He hands them to KENNETH*)

Q: (*as he ties his bow tie*) I had my doubts all along. The public school business has become such a silly specialised system that only the larger preparatory schools really prepare the poor chap for what he has to undergo. Certainly not a tiny school like The Malthouse with a handful of boys and a headmaster who's more like a matron. Waistcoat.

(*KENNETH hands it to him*)

And Rugby is the place of all others where you get the system at full blast, with the least pity. Plenty of kindness from x and y but no pity at all from the system.

(*KENNETH offers him the trousers*)

Not yet. At Eton, Winchester, Wellington even, a toad may dodge the harrow – if you see what I mean – they allow for 'eccentricities' as they call 'em. But Rugby is ruthless, and it's all system. Now – tailcoat. I'll be frank, I'm worried about the boy.

KENNETH: What do you think we should do?

Q: Don't risk another boarding school.

KENNETH: Not even Eton or Winchester?

Q: The boy's too delicate. If I were you I'd send him to Clifton.

KENNETH: Weren't you at Clifton yourself?

Q: Yes, but that's not the point. The great advantage –

(*BADGER enters as 'Rappers', a venerable don in evening dress and sandals*)

RAPPERS: I've brought the hats, Q. I couldn't find any helmets, but I've got the hats.

Q: Rappers and I have been dragooned into appearing in some Gilbert and Sullivan nonsense.

RAPPERS: For our sins.

KENNETH: Grahame.

RAPPERS: Rapson.

(*They shake hands*)

Q: Where was I? Ah yes, Clifton.

RAPPERS: The policemen will simply have to share with the pirates.

Q: Oh do be quiet, Rappers. The great advantage of Clifton is that it's one of the few public schools that accepts day-boys.

RAPPERS: And I've got the swords.

Q: Rappers! Please! 'Course it would mean moving house. And Mrs Grahame would have to surrender the boy totally to the school in term-time. As a day-boy he would only come home to sleep. Would she be prepared to do that?

KENNETH: I very much doubt it.

Q: Then you have no alternative but to abandon the idea of school altogether.

KENNETH: Abandon school? Then what do you suggest?

Q: (*singing to tune of "Modern Major-General" [Music: A.Sullivan]*)
From what I know of dearest Mouse he's not a social animal
And public schoolboys in the raw are verging on the cannibal,

His quaint behaviour loved by us will seem to them quite risible,
They'll give him hell and soon enough he'll wish he were invisible;
I know at home he's noted for his out bursts of loquacity,
A boy of charming humour and exceptional vivacity
But any individual who's just a touch ethereal
Has not a hope of ever being public school material.

KENNETH, RAPPERS:
Has not a hope of ever being public school material (x3)

Q: So send him to a tutor who is well known at the Varsity;
Of private tutors nowadays there really is no sparsity;
I recommend a fellow who's devoid of all severity,
A splendid Oxford blue combining scholarship and levity.

KENNETH, RAPPERS: (*to ELSPETH*)
He recommends a fellow who's devoid of all severity
A splendid Oxford 'blue' combining scholarship and levity.

(*ELSPETH looks unimpressed, so Q continues*)

Q: I know he can be witty and precociously political,
But now you have to face the fact the situation's critical;
Return a 'Toad' to prison, I repeat it most emphatically,
And suddenly his state of mind could alter quite dramatically,
Of course you can pooh-pooh all this and say it's just a patter song –

ELSPETH:
Indeed I do and have to add you've simply got the matter wrong

Q: There's not a public school I know whose rules are not Draconian –

ELSPETH:
The gates of life will open wide if he's an old Etonian!

(*Abrupt end of song*)

KENNETH: Eton?

ALASTAIR: (*entering*) Eton? Won't that be just as bad?

ELSPETH: Bad? It's the best school in the world.

Q: What do you suggest, Rappers?

RAPPERS: Trousers.

(*KENNETH hands trousers to Q. Q and RAPPERS exit*)

KENNETH: Elspeth, listen to me! Are we simply going to ignore Q's advice?

ELSPETH: Yes! – and for one good reason. If going to a private tutor is such a wonderful idea, why didn't Q adopt it for his own son?

KENNETH: Because Bevil was happy at Winchester. Besides he's a very... different kind of boy.

ELSPETH: I don't think Q appreciates the fact that Mouse too has unique talent.

ALASTAIR: Will I have to take Common Entrance again?

ELSPETH: I sincerely hope not. Your father will simply have a word with the headmaster. Won't you, Kenneth?

KENNETH: The war should make things easier.

ELSPETH: In any case you have nothing to fear from Common Entrance. You got into Rugby.

ALASTAIR: Just.

ELSPETH: You passed with flying colours.

KENNETH: That is not so. With all due respect to Mouse, he came very near the bottom of the list. And he was one of the oldest. He clearly does not find examinations easy.

ALASTAIR: Easy? They're agony.

ELSPETH: Well, he's awfully good at games.

ALASTAIR: Ha! Ha!

ELSPETH: Come here, Mouse. (*He goes to her*) Look what I came across the other day. (*Showing him a photograph*) Quite the little cricketer, aren't you? Bat, pads, you look splendid.

ALASTAIR: I can't play cricket for toffee.

ELSPETH: Nonsense. You did awfully well at The Malthouse, all things considered. What were you? I forget.

ALASTAIR: Twelfth man and scorer for the second eleven.

ELSPETH: There you are!

ALASTAIR: In a school of twenty-five? Hardly an achievement.

KENNETH: Q is right, Elspeth. Mouse is not robust. His experience at Rugby proves that.

ELSPETH: I will not have him belittled! – least of all by Q. You're as strong as an ox, my angel. All you need is a little understanding, a little encouragement and plenty of expert tuition. You deserve the best. And the best is Eton.

(*Singing to the tune of "Your King and Country Need You" [Music: P. Rubens]*)

> Oh we don't want to lose you,
> But you must have one more try;
> For boys of ambition never say 'die'.

(*spoken*) Come on, Kenneth!

ELSPETH, KENNETH:

> (*singing*)
> We shall want you and miss you,
> And with all our might and main
> We will cheer you, thank you...

ELSPETH: ... Kiss you

(*ALASTAIR pushes her sharply away*)

(*spoken*) Oh alright.

ELSPETH, KENNETH: (*singing*) Till you come home again!

ELSPETH: His things.

(*KENNETH collects from off-stage, an Eton tailcoat, boater, and a cricket bat*)

Skin a rabbit.

(*ALASTAIR raises his arms in the air, and ELSPETH removes his jumper. Underneath he is wearing an Eton collar etc*)

ELSPETH: That's my boy.

(*Strains of 'Eton Boating Song'. ALASTAIR puts on tailcoat and boater, picks up suitcases and with cricket bat under one arm, moves downstage, as if entering Great Quad at Eton. ELSPETH and KENNETH return to chaise and arm-chair as before. Sound of gun-fire drowning the 'Eton Boating Song'. ALASTAIR places the suitcases end to end in a 'V' formation. Crouches behind them, 'firing' over them with his cricket bat.*)

ELSPETH: Give it everything you've got!

KENNETH: He's surviving!

ELSPETH: What did I tell you?

KENNETH: He's doing better!

ELSPETH: He's been moved up!

(*ALASTAIR stands up, still 'firing' with his cricket bat. ELSPETH and KENNETH applaud*)

ELSPETH/KENNETH: He's in the Remove!

(*ALASTAIR steps out in front of the suitcases*)

ELSPETH: After only a year!

KENNETH: Well played!

(*Applause drowned out by heavy machine-gun fire. ALASTAIR 'firing' from the hip suddenly looks in trouble*)

ELSPETH: Whatever you do, don't slacken now.

KENNETH: He's under tremendous pressure.

ELSPETH: Send reinforcements!

KENNETH: More tuck!

ELSPETH: More money!

ELSPETH/KENNETH: A brand new bicycle!

(*A tremendous explosion. ALASTAIR drops the cricket bat and slumps over the suitcases. BADGER enters as ALASTAIR'S HOUSEMASTER*)

MASTER: Are you alright, Grahame?

(*No response*)

You do get on with the other boys, don't you?

(*No response*)

Is the work too hard for you?

(*No response*)

Grahame, what's wrong?

ALASTAIR: (*Singing to the tune of the First World War song, "I Want To Go Home." [Trad.]*)
> I want to go home,
> I want to go home,
> I'm sick of the blighters who rag me all day,
> I'm sick of a place where I can't have my say;
> I just want to be free,
> Where the bully-boys can't get at me:
> Oh my! I'll try not to cry –
> I want to go home.

MASTER: (*after a slight pause*) I'll ask your father to come and collect you.

(*HOUSEMASTER gives a nod to KENNETH*)

KENNETH: (*helping ALASTAIR up*) Come on, Mouse. I'll take your things.

(HOUSEMASTER and KENNETH help ALASTAIR off-stage with his suitcases etc.)

ELSPETH: *(the old woman again – pulling the frayed cardigan round her shoulders)* I simply do not understand. We gave him everything he wanted. Money, clothes, tuck we could not have done more. Eton – the best school in the world! – I was so disappointed I could hardly bear it. Perhaps we should have sent him to a tutor sooner, but how was one to know? One thought a change of schools would do the trick. Never mind, my darling, you soon recovered. Plenty of swimming and riding with that nice tutor we found you – in no time you were fighting fit again, ready for the challenge of Oxford...

(Lighting change. Spotlight on ALASTAIR)

ALASTAIR: *(to himself)* I don't want to go to Oxford. I want to join the army...go to France. Fight like the others. I love riding and I'm a good horseman. I'll ride to the attack! I'll charge the enemy guns! I'll win medals for bravery – like Bevil Quiller-Couch!

(Lighting change. KENNETH enters with a letter)

KENNETH: Mouse, I've got some good news for you.

ELSPETH: It's so well deserved, my darling.

ALASTAIR: What is it?

KENNETH: You've been offered a place at the House.

ALASTAIR: What house?

KENNETH: Christchurch.

ALASTAIR: Huh.

ELSPETH: Oxford, my darling! Isn't it wonderful?

(ALASTAIR does not respond.)

Your father simply had a word with that cousin of his, didn't you, Kenneth?

KENNETH: The university is so empty they'll be glad of him.

ALASTAIR: I'll join the Volunteers. Noone can stop me doing that.

ELSPETH: Mouse, please!

KENNETH: At Oxford you can always join the Officer Training Corps.

ALASTAIR: The O.T.C. – that's like school. I know what'll happen. The damn war will be over, and I shall have missed it.

ELSPETH: Do stop talking about the war! I don't even want to contemplate your being sent to France.

KENNETH: I shouldn't worry, my dear. I'm sure Mouse will never have to go. Poor chap, with his eyes he wouldn't know a Hun from a Hottentot.

ALASTAIR: I could do *something* surely.

ELSPETH: You *are* going to do something, Mouse. You're going to Oxford.

KENNETH: You lucky chap.

ELSPETH: Your father's green with envy. He never went to Oxford.

ALASTAIR: I thought he was at school there.

KENNETH: School, yes, but not the university.

ALASTAIR: (*to KENNETH hopefully*) Did you fail?

KENNETH: No, I didn't fail. I never had the opportunity. My uncle insisted I go straight into the Bank. (*A slight pause*) It was the biggest disappointment of my life. And the most far-reaching. You see, Mouse, a degree from Oxford or Cambridge isn't just the gateway to the academic life – which was always my dream – but to the professions as well. Without a degree I was stuck at the Bank with no possibility of escape.

ELSPETH: Now do you understand how privileged you are?

(*ALASTAIR does not respond*)

Of course you're a little young, but you're so mature. And it'll give you a head-start over the other boys.

ALASTAIR: How do you mean?

ELSPETH: Well, it means you can pass... whatever it's called – before the others arrive.

KENNETH: F.P.E.

(*Lighting change. Enter RAT, as an OXFORD DON wearing a gown and mortar-board, and carrying a sheaf of question-papers*)

DON: (*announcing*) First Public Examination!

(*BADGER enters as the EXAMINER, also in gown and mortar board*)

EXAMINER: Right! The examination is about to start, and I need hardly remind you that the same discipline applies as in your school examinations. There are two papers: Holy Scripture, and Greek and Latin Literature. You must pass them both in order that you may read for Honours. But take heart: neither paper is difficult. The First Public Examination at this University is, to use a well-worn metaphor, child's play.

(*DON and EXAMINER go to either side of ALASTAIR, who sits down at the desk. DON hands a question-paper to ALASTAIR who peers at it, eyes close to the paper)*

ALASTAIR: (*to himself, as he writes*) March 1918. Holy Scripture.

(*He hands paper to EXAMINER*)

EXAMINER: (*briskly*) Fail.

(*DON hands ALASTAIR another paper*)

ALASTAIR: (*to himself as he writes*) December 1918. Holy Scripture.

(*He hands paper to EXAMINER*)

EXAMINER: Fail.

(*DON hands ALASTAIR another paper*)

ALASTAIR: March 1919. Greek and Latin Literature.

(*He hands paper to EXAMINER*)

EXAMINER: Fail. Pass or Go.

(*DON hands ALASTAIR another paper. The pace is accelerating now*)

ALASTAIR: June 1919. Greek and Latin Literature.

(*He hands paper to EXAMINER*)

EXAMINER: Fail. Grahame A., Christchurch, ceases to be a member of this university. (*ALASTAIR rises*) But may continue to re-sit the examination.

(*ALASTAIR hesitates*)

ELSPETH: Come on, Mouse. It's child's play, remember?

(*ALASTAIR sits. The pace accelerates even more. He hardly has time to peer, let alone write anything*)

ALASTAIR: (*receiving paper*) Holy Scrip....

EXAMINER: (*taking it*) Fail.

ALASTAIR: (*receiving paper*) Greek and Lat...

EXAMINER: (*taking it*) Fail. (*Taking ALASTAIR'S pen. More slowly*) In future examinations application may be made for an amanuensis, as in the case of blind students.

(*DON hands ALASTAIR another paper*)

ALASTAIR: March 1920. Greek and Latin Literature.

EXAMINER: Pass.

ALASTAIR: Pass?

EXAMINER: Pass.

(*Bells ring out joyfully. The stage is flooded with light. DON (RAT) goes to piano. ELSPETH and KENNETH rise. ALASTAIR sinks back exhausted. EXAMINER continues to stand over him*)
(*SONG to the tune of "Me and My Gal" [Music: George W. Meyer]*)

ELSPETH: The bells are ringing for marvellous Mouse!

KENNETH: The birds are singing for marvellous Mouse!

ELSPETH, KENNETH:
                 Everybody's been knowing

ELSPETH: That his worth he'd be showing;

KENNETH: I admit she is crowing. My excitable spouse!

ELSPETH, KENNETH:
                 We're celebrating for Marvellous Mouse!
                 The world is waiting for Marvellous Mouse!

ELSPETH: And very soon he'll show the world a thing.
                 Or two, or three or four or more,

ELSPETH, KENNETH:
                 So drink now to marvellous Mouse!

(*End of Song*)

EXAMINER: I hate to dampen your spirits, but he still has to pass Scripture.

ELSPETH: A formality.

DON: After three attempts?

ALASTAIR: May I now return to my rooms in College?

EXAMINER: Alas, no. Until you have passed the First Public Examination 'in toto', you will not be re-admitted as a member of this college or university. You must therefore remain in lodgings, but may dine in hall, if you so wish. You may of course continue to re-sit the examination.

(*To DON as they start to exit*)

Two years over F.P.E.!

DON: Must be a record.

(*DON and EXAMINER exit*)

ELSPETH: (*to ALASTAIR*) Now at last your foot is on the ladder. Do not take it off again.

ALASTAIR: I still haven't passed scripture. Without Scripture I haven't passed F.P.E.

ELSPETH: Mount it steadily rung by rung.

ALASTAIR: Without F.P.E. I haven't even started.

ELSPETH: The next step is an Honours Degree.

ALASTAIR: The next step is to pass Scripture.

ELSPETH: Come on, Mouse, cheer up. Scripture is your favourite subject.

ALASTAIR: I loathe Scripture.

ELSPETH: But you're my little mystic. Have you forgotten your friend 'The Carpenter'? He was your first pal.

ALASTAIR: I don't have any pals.

ELSPETH: Nonsense!

ALASTAIR: Besides I don't believe any more.

ELSPETH: Darling! You've grown up.

ALASTAIR: You haven't the smallest particle of understanding, have you.

KENNETH: Mouse! Look, I've got something for you.

ALASTAIR: What is it?

KENNETH: Come and see.

(*ALASTAIR goes to KENNETH, who hands him a large book*)

ALASTAIR: "Cruden's Concordance." What's this for?

KENNETH: Well it's a religious dictionary.

ALASTAIR: I know that!

KENNETH: I had it sent specially – to help you with your Scripture.

ALASTAIR: As if a dictionary can solve anything.

(*He discards the book on the nearest available surface*)

ELSPETH: What did your tutor have to say, Mouse? Was he helpful?

ALASTAIR: He said my handwriting had improved.

ELSPETH: (*after a slight pause*) Well, what does it matter? All that matters is that you've passed that beastly exam, and now you will go on from strength to strength. Oh Kenneth, I'm so thrilled! We'll celebrate! We'll invite all our friends!

KENNETH: We don't have any friends.

ELSPETH: We'll play the gramophone! One of our old favourites. Mouse, you shall choose. Let's dance.

(*Sound of dance music. She swirls round the room with an imaginary partner*)

ELSPETH: Come on, Mouse. You must join in. You're the one we're celebrating. You're the one who...

(*The music stops abruptly. ALASTAIR lies down in the middle of the stage*)

ELSPETH: (*sharply*) Mouse, what are you doing?

KENNETH: Get up out of the road, there's a good fellow.

ELSPETH: It's not a road, it's a railway line!

(*Very faintly, in the distance, the sound of a steam train. It approaches, nearer and nearer, as the following speeches crescendo*)

ALASTAIR: I am Toad once more.

KENNETH: I can see it clearly now! It's an engine, on our rails! Coming along at a great pace!

ALASTAIR: Toad the Terror!

ELSPETH: Get up, get up! You'll be killed!

KENNETH: They're gaining on us fast!

ALASTAIR: Lord of the Lone Trail!

KENNETH: The engine is crowded with people, all waving, all shouting!

ELSPETH: Stop!

KENNETH: Stop!

ELSPETH: (*screaming*) STOP!

(*She covers her face in horror. Blackout. The train thunders past. Silence. Lights come slowly up. ELSPETH is sitting on her chaise, with KENNETH beside her. BADGER as the CORONER and RAT as the MEDICAL OFFICER are as if in a Coroner's Court*)

MED. OFFICER: On the evening of 7th May Alastair Grahame, a commoner of Christchurch, Oxford, dined in hall as usual. After the meal he asked for a glass of port – which, according to a fellow undergraduate, he had never done before. Then – it was not yet dark – he went for a solitary walk across Port Meadow. It was the last time he was seen alive.

CORONER: Was the body between the rails?

MED. OFFICER: Yes, in the four-foot way of the down line. The cause of death was decapitation. The right arm was fractured below the shoulder, the left leg four inches above the ankle, the right leg just above the ankle, and all the toes of the right foot. There were also numerous bruises on the body due to abrasure by projecting parts of the engines and trains as they passed over him. Six trains passed the spot between 10pm and 2.45am, when the body was found.

CORONER: Are these injuries compatible with being knocked down by a train and then run over?

MED. OFFICER: I could not answer the first part of the question as to being knocked down, but certainly they are compatible with being run over.

CORONER: I have not summoned the parents, but you saw them, did you not?

MED. OFFICER: Yes.

CORONER: And they told you, I think, that the lad was physically weak and had always been so?

MED. OFFICER: Yes.

CORONER: That he was blind in one eye from birth?

MED. OFFICER: Yes.

CORONER: And never indulged in games?

MED. OFFICER: Never to my knowledge.

CORONER: And the family relationship between him and them was of the happiest?

MED.OFFICER: Yes.

CORONER: That is what the parents said?

MED.OFFICER: Yes.

CORONER: Gentlemen, this is a case of the saddest type. A young man, the only son of his parents, with every comfort, on the best of terms with his parents, without trouble, either financial or any other, suddenly loses his life. Now it is quite obvious that an occurrence of this sort might be due to one of two things. It might be due to a deliberate attempt on the part of the person to destroy himself. And in this case it must be admitted that the injuries described by the Medical Officer allow the possibility that the deceased may have been already lying on the rails when he was run over. That is to say, he may and I stress 'may', have deliberately laid himself down in a slightly diagonal position, his neck and left shoulder on one rail, his right foot and left leg on the other – and waited. I have spelled this out, because I submit that such an act is inconceivable without the strongest motive. And in this case obviously there was no motive whatever. The only things found in his pockets were a few religious tracts, which is hardly surprising since he was studying theology. And there was nothing left in his lodgings to show any anxiety or trouble in his life. Friday evening was dark, as I happen to know because I was out late. If a man somewhat blind, physically weak, went out for a walk and by some chance got on the railway line – even though he was near a level crossing and even though it was an area he must have known well by day – at night it would be a dangerous place; an accident might well occur. I leave you to consider your verdict.

(*Exit CORONER and MEDICAL OFFICER. Lighting change. ELSPETH is sitting peering at a newspaper. KENNETH has moved away and stands looking blankly in front of him*)

ELSPETH: (*suddenly*) There! That proves it. There it is in black and white – for all to see. How dare anyone suggest now that it was not an accident!

KENNETH: It's only a rumour.

ELSPETH: People are *hateful*, even your friend Q...

KENNETH: I'll write to him and explain what must have happened. I know the place well. (*A wry afterthought*) We used to play cricket on Port Meadow....

ELSPETH: (*tearful*) Poor little mite! To think of him suffering like that..

(*KENNETH goes to her and puts his arm round her*)

Those horrible, horrible injuries... take the newspaper away!

(*KENNETH takes the newspaper and hides it away in the drawer of the table*)

KENNETH: At least he's free now.

ELSPETH: Free from what?

KENNETH: Prison.

ELSPETH: What are you talking about?

KENNETH: He once said, didn't he, "This life is a prison." Like Toad, he's finally made his escape.

ELSPETH: (*after a slight pause*) He was too good for this world. He came down to us for a little while, inspired that beautiful book – and departed. D'you remember that wonderful thing he said when he was just a little chap? He said to Nanny – and he can't have been a day over four – he said "Death is Promotion".

KENNETH: It's a beautiful day. Why don't we sit outside and have lunch in the garden?

ELSPETH: There's only a chicken leg.

KENNETH: We'll share it. And I'll open a bottle of port.

(*In the distance, children's voices singing [Music: J. Stainer]:-*

> There's a Friend for little children
> Above the bright blue sky,
> A Friend who never changes
> Whose love can never die:
> Unlike our friends by nature,
> Who change with passing years,
> This Friend is always worthy
> The precious name he bears.

Meanwhile ELSPETH produces the chicken leg from the paper bag and starts to eat. KENNETH rises, crosses to the picnic hamper and gets out a bottle of port and two glasses. They sit on the floor by the hamper. He pours out two glasses of port and hands one to her. The children's hymn fades out)

ELSPETH: Dino!

KENNETH: Minkie!

(*They clink glasses. He kisses her lightly.*)

ELSPETH: To us.

KENNETH: I'm going to take you on a long holiday.

ELSPETH: Holiday? Where?

KENNETH: Italy.

ELSPETH: Italy! Oh Dino, am I allowed to share your beloved Italy?

(*He nods. She hugs him.*)

We'll go there every year!

KENNETH: More often if we want to.

ELSPETH: I can't wait to gorge myself on that heavenly architecture.

KENNETH: I can't wait to gorge myself on that heavenly ice-cream.

ELSPETH: Now be careful, Dino. Too much ice-cream is bad for the heart.

KENNETH: You know, I've started to write again.

ELSPETH: You haven't!

KENNETH: Only a short tribute to Keats. Nothing too demanding.

ELSPETH: We'll move house. Find somewhere smaller, cosier, (*romantically*) just right for two...

KENNETH: What about his things?

ELSPETH: What things?

KENNETH: His clothes... his cricket-bat.

ELSPETH: Give them to the jumble sale. I want to drink a toast. Refill my glass.

(*He does so. She raises her glass*)

The Listener!

KENNETH: Who?

ELSPETH: The little night-gowned boy!

KENNETH: Oh yes.

ELSPETH: (*crossing to the chaise*) Without such a listener there would never have been such a story.

KENNETH: I feel strangely tired.

(*She puts on her dressing-gown and sits on her chaise*)

ELSPETH: Without him there would have been no Toad, no Badger, no Ratty...

(*Enter RAT, as RAT again, dressed in yachting cap etc*)

RAT: (*going to KENNETH who is now becoming MOLE again*) I feel just as you do, Mole. Simply dead tired, though not body-tired.

MOLE: I feel, Ratty, as if I had been through something very exciting and rather terrible, and it was just over.

RAT: It's lucky we've got the stream with us, to take us home.

(*Distant music – 'Down By The Willows' from 'Toad Of Toad Hall' [H. Fraser-Simson]) – as RAT collects the bottle and glasses, replaces them in the hamper and closes it.*)

MOLE: (*rising*) It's like music – far-away music. What is it?

RAT: Only the wind playing in the reeds.

MOLE: (*starting to go*) What does it say? I can't catch the words.

RAT: (*casually*) It says "Forget, forget."

(*He goes to the French windows and closes the curtains. He picks up the hamper and exits with MOLE.*

The room is now as it was at the opening. No light except for the dingy standard lamp. ELSPETH, who has dozed off on her chaise, wakes with a start)

ELSPETH: Dino! Dino, where are you? (*She looks towards the empty armchair*) You just slipped away, didn't you...one night without warning...as if on tiptoe... leaving me alone.... (*Slight pause*) How can I forget? Where did I put that Parker woman's letter? (*Rummages*) There was something she said I should do...some advice..... (*She finds the letter and skims through it*) What was it? Ah (*Reading*) "Try writing something down, something you..." God! Her handwriting!... "particularly want to hear from them. Burn it, and wait for the answer, which may come in some form or other..."

(*She gathers a piece of paper, a pencil, a box of matches and a plate*)

Dino!... Are you listening?...Are you there?...I'm going to ask you a question. The question you and I shared for so long – ever since...A question we never asked, because the answer had been given in a court of law. But secretly... I... perhaps you...Dino, put my mind at rest.

(*She writes for a moment, puts the paper on the plate and sets light to it. As the paper burns*)

It was an accident – wasn't it?

(*Lights slowly fade to blackout*)